CoolGlobes

Cool Globes Exhibit Steering Committee

Wendy Abrams, Chairwoman
William Abrams
Nancy Bank
Lisa Fremont
Karen Frey
De Gray
Amanda Hanley
Lynn Harris
Bob Kallen
Shelly Kielar
Anne Loucks
Lucy Moog
Amy Krause Rosenthal
Karen Segal
Cathy Stein
John Woldenberg

Published by Imagination Publishing
Jim Meyers, President
© 2007

ISBN 978-0-9763245-2-2

Printed in Canada by Friesens

Mohawk Environmental Savings
Printed on Mohawk Options Recycled, which is made from 100% post-consumer waste fiber.
The carbon emissions from all of the energy used to produce these papers is offset with Green-e certified, wind-generated electricity and purchased Verified Emissions Reduction credits (VERs), making it entirely carbon neutral.

By printing this book on Mohawk Options Recycled, the following environmental savings were realized:
200.02 trees preserved for the future
577.57 pounds of water-borne waste not created
84,962 gallons of wastewater flow saved
9,401 pounds of solid waste not generated
18,510 pounds net of greenhouse gases prevented 141,678,000 BTUs of energy not consumed
9,617 pounds of air emissions not generated and 4 barrels of crude oil unused

This is equivalent to not driving 10,418 miles in an average car or to planting 650 trees.

contents

To my parents, the most thoughtful and giving people on the planet;
to David, Emily, Katie & Jake—my inspirations;
and to Jimmy, who has the miraculous ability
to keep me grounded while helping me fly—I love you.

"I had a dream where we help the world"

—KATIE ABRAMS, AGE 5

Richard M. Daley
Mayor, City of Chicago

The City of Chicago is proud to sponsor Cool Globes, a community-wide effort, uniting corporate, government and non-profit organizations. Designed to inform and inspire people to take action against global warming, this public art exhibit educates each of us on what we can do to address this serious problem.

A group of scientists from 113 countries issued a report recently that said global warming will cause rising sea levels, more powerful storms, both floods and droughts. But you don't have to read a scientific report to see the impact of global warming. Last summer was the hottest on record and the average yearly temperature was the highest ever. Two years ago, we in the United States had some of the worst hurricanes in history. Entire lakes in Asia and Africa have practically disappeared and so have some of the world's most majestic glaciers.

We all share responsibility for global warming. We all can be part of the solution.

Cool Globes is another example of Chicago's national leadership in protecting the environment. We strive to be the greenest city in America. Our city has planted hundreds of thousands of trees; has built or plans to build healthy, cost-effective green libraries, police and fire stations and public schools; and has shifted to fuel-efficient hybrid vehicles for city use.

The Cool Globes project embodied the vision, environmental awareness and beauty that define Chicago. I am truly proud that the City of Chicago served as a partnering sponsor, and I hope the public enjoyed this exhibit and all Chicago has to offer. It was an honor to host Cool Globes in our city.

ripple effect

1 committment to the Clinton Global Initiative

29 members of Cool Globes Advisory Board—including 6 heads of environmental organizations

72 volunteers on the Cool Globes Executive Committee who contributed approximately 18,000 volunteer hours over 58 weeks

125 sponsors—including 110 corporations, 12 foundations, 1 synagogue, and 24 individuals

130 artists of large globes

250 mini-globes decorated by celebrities including 1 former first lady, 4 Senators, 1 astronaut, 3 blue men, 26 athletes and 18 rock stars

100's of school children participating in the "Cool Globes by Cool Kids" educational program

1,200 people at an opening gala and 1,000 at the mini-globes silent auction

50 trained docents led hundreds of tours for thousands of people

35 schools that will expose approximately 35,000 students in 2007 to curricula on global warming developed by Cool Globes in partnership with the Chicago Public Schools

100,000 Cool Globes guidebooks printed and distributed throughout Chicago via Starbucks & Whole Foods

More than **$4** million in sponsorship and in-kind donations

millions of people of all ages who saw the Cool Globes in Chicago in the summer of 2007

0 carbon footprint

preface

by President William J. Clinton

Across our planet, temperatures are rising, bringing severe climate patterns that endanger our future. In the face of this challenge, we can do nothing and allow our children to inherit an even greater crisis, or we each can play a role in building a sustainable future for them, by working together with our creativity, capital and connections, to transform our ideas into action.

That's why I established the Clinton Global Initiative (CGI): to convene a diverse group of leaders from around the world, to devise and implement innovative, effective solutions to some of the world's most pressing issues. Now entering its third year, CGI is producing terrific results in improving health, reducing poverty, combating climate change, and other areas. Wendy Abrams' commitment in 2006—to facilitate "public art with a purpose"—exemplifies how one person, armed with a great idea, can inspire others to work for change.

Wendy will tell you she's just a mom who became increasingly concerned about global warming and the risks it posed to her children. Even so, after participating in CGI in 2006, Wendy began to take action: she reached out to friends and colleagues, and contributed her time and financial resources, all to help bring attention to the climate change crisis. Before long, Wendy launched Cool Globes: 124 uniquely decorated spheres gracing the City of Chicago, on display for millions of people. Each Cool Globe illustrates one way to step up and help stop global warming.

Cool Globes reflects the essence of the Clinton Global Initiative. By fostering openness to new ideas and partners, and encouraging measurable action, CGI has—in two years—inspired almost 600 commitments, impacting over 1,000 organizations in 100 countries. Wendy calls CGI's impact a "ripple effect." In the summer of 2007, the ripples of Lake Michigan reflected the artistry of Cool Globes and the power of inspiration. In future seasons, our shared capacity to change the world can create ripples that have no bounds.

the making of cool globes

by Wendy Abrams

I never considered myself an environmentalist. To me, an environmentalist was a guy in a raft protesting to save the whales as he drifted in the Pacific. But in 2001, that changed when I casually stumbled upon a *Time* magazine article about global warming, depicting potentially catastrophic consequences within the century. As a mother of four, this hit a nerve—the next century is my children's lifetime. I was suddenly motivated to act and spent the next five years educating myself by joining environmental groups, attending conferences, meeting with scientists and becoming engaged in the political debate.

The more I learned, the more I was bewildered by the discrepancy between the scientific community's alarm and the general public's silence. The public seemed relatively unconcerned by the scientists' daunting predictions, if they were even aware of the predictions at all. The American press showed disproportionately little interest in covering global warming, given the magnitude of the problem. And even when the press did cover the story, studies showed that many people tuned out the subject because they felt overwhelmed by the problem and helpless as to the solutions.

I was intrigued by the question of how to capture the public's attention on a subject as complex as global warming. One night, in a casual discussion with friends, we came up with an idea—"public art with a purpose." The idea was to put sculptures on the sidewalk, each depicting a solution to global warming, forcing people to confront the issue, but in a non-threatening manner.

As a participant at the 2006 Clinton Global Initiative, I was asked to make a commitment to take action. With the incentive to return to the next annual conference, I put my pledge in writing. I committed to raise awareness of global warming using the medium of public art, and established the non-profit organization, Cool Globes Inc.

I began by enlisting two of the most competent and well respected people in Chicago: John McCarter, president of The Field Museum, and the Environmental Commissioner, Sadhu Johnston. Fortunately—after a bit of persistent persuasion—both agreed to partner on this project: the Cool Globes: Hot Ideas for a Cooler Planet exhibit. We established an Advisory Board and Executive Committee, and I approached business leaders, environmental leaders, elected officials, community leaders, artists and educators. Surprisingly, all agreed to serve. What I discovered was that this was an issue that people were eager to address, particularly when we mentioned the emphasis on solutions.

Over the next year, I experienced something truly inspiring. People whom I had never met prior to this project devoted themselves entirely to Cool Globes. It became a full-time, non-paying job. It wasn't an easy job, or a predictable job.

supplemental efforts

As our primary goal was to raise awareness of global warming, we expanded our efforts beyond the art exhibit with several supplemental programs.
• In April, 2007, Cool Globes held the "Cool Globes by Cool Kids" contest. Schoolchildren throughout Chicago created their own globes decorated to depict solutions to global warming. Winners were selected by the City of Chicago's Department of Environment and Mayor Daley presented awards to the schoolchildren during Chicago's Earth Day Celebration 2007.

• In partnership with Chicago Public Schools and the Peggy Notebaert Nature Museum, Cool Globes developed a multidisciplinary education program for 6th graders, focusing on global warming solutions. The new curriculum will be introduced to thousands of schoolchildren beginning in the 2007-2008 schoolyear.
• Cool Globes enlisted the help of politicians, rock stars, athletes, schoolchildren and even an astronaut to decorate miniature globes. The message of this supplemental exhibit—everyone cares about global warming.

The mini-globes were exhibited at Sears Tower and the Hancock Center. A series of mini-globes were also exhibited at the United Nations in New York in celebration of World Environment Day.
• On July 11th, Cool Globes hosted a Business Leaders Roundtable at Northwestern University's Kellogg Graduate School of Management. The one-day conference provided a forum for senior executives and environmental leaders to come together and share ideas for addressing climate change.

Together we scrambled to solve problems that arose. We realized, for instance, that the five-foot diameter globes were too wide to fit through the doors of many artists' studios. We found donated warehouse space and created "Camp Cool Globes." Volunteers gave up weekends, evenings, even Easter was spent proof-reading plaques due Monday morning at the engraver.

The enthusiasm extended beyond the committee. Sponsors took a risk on this project. We had no track record. We didn't even have the actual globes to present, only artists' sketchy renditions of what they planned to create. And yet, again, there was an incredible outpouring of support which I can only attribute to the cause—an eagerness to embrace solutions to global warming. Originally, we

anticipated an exhibition of 25 globes; in the end, we had five times that many.

The artists began crafting their enormous blank canvases, many working in the chilly warehouse space that was warm with camaraderie. It was exciting to see the blank globes being brought to life in a wide array of mediums, showcasing an even wider array of solutions. From the elaborate mosaics and

artists _{speak}..

Matt Binns is re-shaping the face of global warming, one globe at a time. The talented sculptor specializing in building aluminum globes up to 8' in diameter designed the original Cool Globes mold.
"Using a variety of techniques and tools

derived from armourers and blacksmiths of the 18th century—along with lots of elbow grease and bad language—we wrestle flat materials into delightful curves," Binn says.

detailed paintings, to the 34 pounds of parachute chord that Lindsay Obermeyer spent months knitting into a sweater (reminding us to turn down the thermostat) to Lisa Fedich's globe covered in pinwheels painted by Lisa's young, hospitalized students. The artwork was as spectacular as it was diverse.

At the same time, behind the scenes, law firms, ad agencies, logistics firms, trucking companies were all working tirelessly, as the June 1 opening approached. In the end, in-kind donations outstripped monetary donations.

On June 1, Mayor Richard M. Daley unveiled the Cool Globes: Hot Ideas for a Cooler Planet Exhibit on the city's Museum Campus. The overcast sky cleared and sunshine smiled on the hundreds of artists, sponsors, schoolchildren and guests who were in attendance to celebrate.

Throughout the summer I have had the pleasure of strolling the exhibit and watching people of all ages enjoy the globes. Toddlers run up to the globes, bikers stop to read the plaques, parents walk about explaining the virtues of recycling to their children. When people ask me if Cool Globes has been a success, I don't think about the sponsorship contributions or the sell-out crowd at the gala, but I look at the faces of the people who see the globes, and I am proud to have been one person, among many, who brought this project to fruition.

what is global warming

The science is clear: the earth is warming at an unprecedented rate, and carbon dioxide emissions from human activity are largely responsible for the rapid change. To put it simply, carbon dioxide and other gases such as methane, trap infrared rays from the sun in the atmosphere and warm the earth. While some heat-trapping gases are natural and have allowed us to enjoy a planet with a moderate climate, the dramatic rise in atmospheric CO_2 is causing alarm among the scientific community.

Scientists have been measuring the carbon dioxide levels in the atmosphere for much of the past century, observing a significant rise in CO_2 levels in recent decades—not surprising as coal-burning power plants and automobiles produce 4 billion tons of carbon dioxide every year in the U.S. alone. Scientists are able to compare CO_2 measurements to historic data obtained by drilling deep into the ice cores at the North and South Poles—providing insight into the planet's climate history for the past 650,000 years.

While there have been shifts in climate throughout history, the shifts have occurred at a very slow rate—usually over periods of several thousand years—allowing species to evolve and adapt to the changes. What we are currently witnessing is a dramatic increase in carbon dioxide levels in the atmosphere, due to burning of fossil fuels and the destruction of forests which absorb carbon. The current rate of change is much faster than ever before.

Left unchecked, the world's leading climatologists project a rise in average global temperatures of 3 to 11 degrees Fahrenheit within the century. To put this in perspective, scientists state that a 9 degree shift would make the Earth largely uninhabitable.

The consequences of global warming are serious: changing weather patterns, more frequent and more severe storms, rising sea levels and melting glaciers. Warmer temperatures mean more drought, more floods, higher food prices, even higher insurance premiums. Melting glaciers and diminishing snow pack will mean shortfall in water supplies, impacting everyone from farmers and municipalities to ski resorts and trout fisherman. Rising sea levels will impact nearly every coastal city in the world—forcing people from their homes and creating

millions of refugees from low-lying countries such as Bangladesh and the Netherlands.

While the challenge of global warming is great, the opportunity is even greater. We have renewable energy sources to reduce, even eliminate our dependence on fossil fuels. Energy efficiency and conservation will not only result in lower carbon emissions, but also lower expenditures. Developing new technologies means the opportunity for job creation, economic growth, a cleaner environment and a higher standard of living.

There is, now more than ever, a need to raise awareness of the dangers associated with global warming; a need to illuminate the opportunity to develop a cleaner, sustainable future for generations to come. Solving this global challenge will require leadership from government, corporate and community leaders. It will also require personal responsibility from individuals. We can all be part of the solution.

hottest **years**

"The findings are powerful: the 10 in recorded history have all occurred since 1990."

"It doesn't make sense for us to sit back and wait for others to **act.** The fate of our **planet** that our children and grandchildren will inherit is **in our hands** and it is our responsibility to do something about this **crisis.**"

—PRESIDENT BILL CLINTON

personal responsibility

"Think of it: if every household in America replaced just one box of tissues with recycled tissues, about

1,630,

Over the past 35 years, personal waste has doubled from 2.7 pounds to 4.4 pounds per day.

27% of our food supply—97 billion pounds—went to waste in 1995.

Recycling one aluminum can saves enough electricity to power a television or a 100-watt bulb for three hours.

Recycle.

1. Americans (consumers and industry) throw away enough aluminum in one year to rebuild our entire commercial airplane fleet every three months.
2. The average baby uses 10,000 diapers before toilet training. One billion trees are used each year to produce disposable diapers.
3. Every ton of paper recycled saves 17 trees.

Organic waste takes up 1/3 of landfill space.

trees would be saved each year. **"**

the **change** you wish to **see**

"Self-Reflection" MICKI LEMIEUX

It is understandable for one person to feel overwhelmed by the daunting task of solving global warming; to wonder— **"What can I do?** What difference does it make anyhow?"

Look in the mirror. Take a minute and **think about your daily actions** and the **impact your actions have on the planet**. Everything from the houses we live in, the cars we drive, even the food we eat... **the choices we make** in nearly every aspect of our lives **have an impact on the planet** and the footprint we leave.

But therein lies the answer—it is the things that one individual can do that matter most. You are the difference. Without each one of us, nothing changes.

The United States ranks as the #1 global warming polluter in the world per capita.
—Environmental Defense

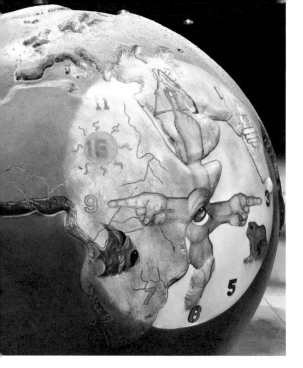

Artists Speak

Everyone can do something. And it doesn't have to be difficult or expensive to implement. Even the simplest actions make a difference. Whether you choose to improve the energy efficiency of your home, carpool, become a more environmentally conscious consumer or simply walk and bike more, you can reduce or neutralize your carbon footprint.

Change Your Perspective

Clearly, people are consuming goods and services at an unsustainable pace. This reality has serious consequences for the well-being of human beings and the planet. Consequently, we're beginning to ask ourselves questions that are small, but important and incremental.

- Why throw something away if it can be recycled or reused?
- Why drive if public transportation, a carpool or a bike is available?
- Why print something when you have the electronic file?
- Why not shop with companies that are making green, eco-friendly products, which would then encourage them to be even more environmentally responsible?

notes 7 WAYS TO REDUCE ENERGY CONSUMPTION

1. Turn off water when brushing teeth.
2. Unplug cell phone charger when not in use.
3. Shut down computer at night.

4. Use a manual can opener.
5. Adjust your thermostat 1° higher in the summer and 1° lower in the winter.
6. Drive one mile slower.

7. Replace one light bulb in a closet with an energy saving fluorescent bulb.

—source: teeniegreenie.org

Change Your Perspective

Romero Britto's work figures in some of the great international art collections and has been displayed in museum exhibits around the world. He has collaborated with other famed artists such as Andy Warhol with whom he created a limited edition bottle for Absolut Vodka. Britto literally turned the world on its head in his globe because changing how we see the Earth is the only way to save it.

Artists Speak

Stop Unsolicited Mail
Ellen Gradman collected junk mail from 36 families for one week. The result: 100 pounds of unsolicited mail that she used to give her globe its "trashy" appearance.

Stop Unsolicited Mail

The average American receives the equivalent of 1.5 trees in their mailbox every year in the form of unsolicited mail. That adds up to more than 100 million trees cut down and more than 28 billion gallons of water consumed. Reducing the amount of junk mail you receive saves energy, natural resources and landfill space.

Contact the Direct Marketing Association and ask to be removed from mass market mailing lists. Call the toll-free numbers in unwanted catalogs and ask to be removed from mailing lists.

Artists Speak

Self Reflection
Micki LeMieux graduated from the School of Art Institute of Chicago and has been working as a sculptor ever since, creating works for organizations such as NBC, Levi Strauss, the Lyric Opera of Chicago and Steppenwolf Theatre. LeMieux's work has appeared in multiple outdoor parks and been showcased in many solo and group exhibitions around the United States. LeMieux's self-reflection globe was achieved by using mirror-like paints, conveying the message that it is now time to view the earth and the individual as one.

12 "Americans throw away enough paper annually to build a wall **feettall** from New York City to Los Angeles."

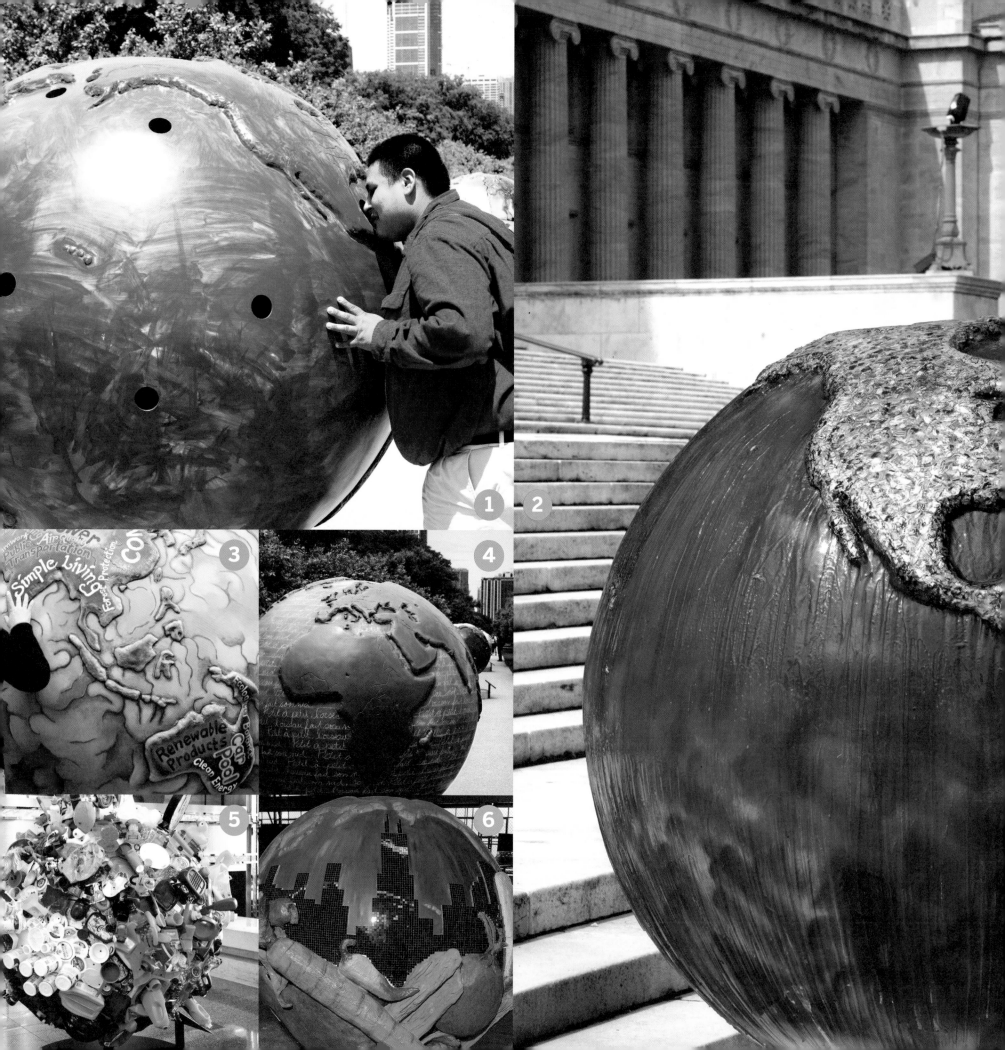

Artists Speak

● 1. Learn From Ecology

Filled with real plants, Stockyard Institute and Hyde Park Art Center's globe represents the delicate environment in which we live. "We are committed to engaging the questions of our youth and residents through education, activism and media."

● 2. Buy Recycled

Gregory Warmack, better known as 'Mr. Imagination', is a self-taught artist who began his career by selling his work on the streets of Chicago. He collected objects such as rocks and beads and used his found material to create jewelry that he sold to passersby. Since then, his unique creations have become coveted pieces of art and his background in reusing materials came in handy when he crafted his Cool Globe. Mr. Imagination covered his continents with differently shaped flattened bottle caps and the oceans out of glossy paints. When spectators look at the shiny surfaces they can see their own reflections as a reminder that each of us must do our part in order to save our planet.

● 3. Consumer Power

Knowledge is key, according to Ken Klopak. In Klopak's artistic vision, the globe is a brain, emphasizing the importance of educating consumers around the world. "With the participation of all the peoples of the world, we will find many effective ways to solve the environmental problems affecting our world, developing a promising legacy for other generations to follow," says Klopak.

● 4. Green Products

"Little by little, the bird builds its nest," is the saying that circles the globe created by Gardiner C. Funo O'Kain. It is written in French on the surface, which is also a green chalkboard, stressing the importance of education and the promise of innovation.

● 5. Reduce

Yair Engel is an Israeli citizen who came to the U.S. specifically to contribute his artwork to the Cool Globes project. His globe is cluttered with bulky, extraneous packaging to show the importance of choosing products with recyclable packaging. With the average person accumulating 2.5 pounds of trash every day, this globe lets viewers know that it is time to make a change.

● 6. Buy Local

Buying food that is grown locally is not only good for your health but also the health of the environment. Eliza Browne's globe displays a city skyline surrounded by oversized fruits and vegetables. This piece of art suggests that you don't have to live in the country to buy from your local growers. Produce would taste a lot better knowing that the trip it took to get to your mouth was short and saved much-needed transportation energy.

A "carbon footprint" is defined as the amount of carbon dioxide released as a result of your daily activities. Lifestyle choices, household energy usage and transportation methods all affect the size of your "footprint."

The average U.S. citizen's carbon footprint is 19 tons of CO_2 per year, making Americans the largest contributors of greenhouse gas emissions. In contrast, per capita emissions in the United Kingdom are less then half at 9.1 tons. The average carbon footprint in China is only 4.7 tons of CO_2.

Artists Speak

Be Responsible

The weight of the world is on our shoulders but with more people helping, the load could get a little lighter. Christopher Campagna's globe depicts the strenuous task of Atlas carrying the world on his back much as each of us carries the health of our environment. All of humankind has the responsibility to care for the future of our planet collectively.

"It is now time to view the **earth** and the **individual** as one."

measure your footprint

Every mile you fly emits 0.64 pounds of carbon dioxide.

Flight miles per year _____
x .64
= Year Total _____

Various types of home heating emit different amounts of carbon dioxide. Home heating oil emits the most; electricity the least.

Electricity per year (kilowatt hours) _____ **x 1.34**
= Year Total _____

The average car gets 20 miles per gallon, which equals about one pound of carbon dioxide per mile.

Miles driven per year _____
x 1
= Year Total _____

Every time you tumble dry clothes in a dryer, carbon dioxide is emitted. In fact, 90 dryer cycles produce 1 ton of carbon dioxide, or 1000 kilograms.

11.1 kg x _____ **Number of dryer loads per year**
= _____ **Mkg of carbon dioxide emitted each year**

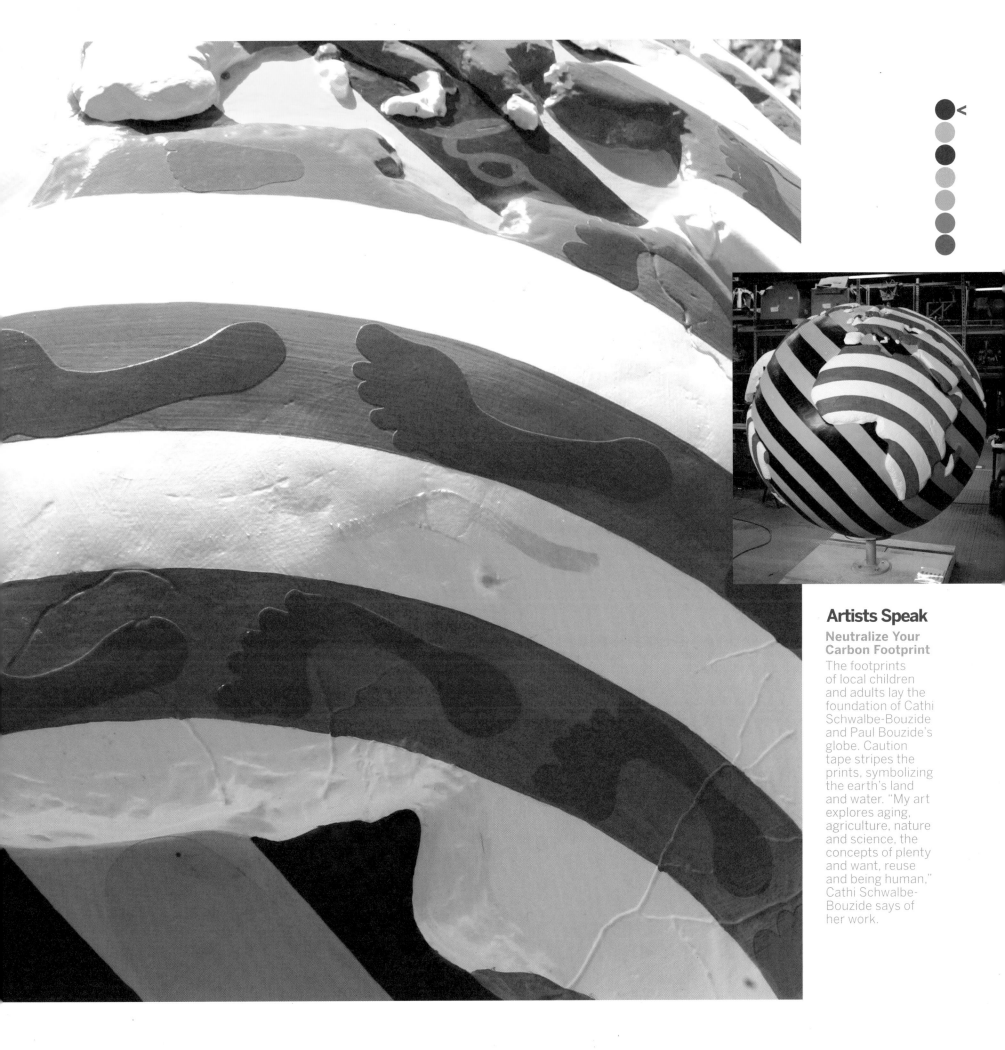

Artists Speak

Neutralize Your Carbon Footprint

The footprints of local children and adults lay the foundation of Cathi Schwalbe-Bouzide and Paul Bouzide's globe. Caution tape stripes the prints, symbolizing the earth's land and water. "My art explores aging, agriculture, nature and science, the concepts of plenty and want, reuse and being human," Cathi Schwalbe-Bouzide says of her work.

carbon neutrality

Climate change is a global problem, so reducing emissions anywhere on the planet has the same positive effect as cutting back locally. In other words, you can pay someone else to reduce your emissions. Organizations and companies that produce eco-friendly energy, such as wind farms and solar installations, sell "carbon offsets." In effect, it's an exchange that lets you credit your carbon footprint with a reduction in your emissions.

With carbon offsets, everybody wins. If you buy an offset at a wind energy company, for instance, you're purchasing new non-polluting energy. The wind energy company benefits because it can sell its non-polluting energy at a lower cost to other customers.

Calculating and managing your carbon emissions efficiently also prepares you for the inevitable: In the not too distant future, carbon dioxide and other greenhouse gases are likely to be regulated and taxed.

In the meantime, you can become "carbon neutral," a goal we should all set for ourselves. Carbon neutrality is perhaps the easiest way to meet your personal responsibility for a cleaner Earth. In fact, carbon neutrality has become so popular—and so important—that it was selected as the New Oxford Dictionary's 2006 "Word of the Year."

It is not a substitute for actually reducing your own emissions in ways such as driving less, conserving energy at home and at work, and recycling, but it supports the growth of the renewable energy industry and helps make us more energy independent.

artists speak ....

Calculate Your Carbon Footprint

"Life on earth is a gift. Unique in our known universe, our planet is an environment conducive to breath. I chose renewable energy as a theme for the globe because I am awed by the power of the natural world, as well as marvel at the infinite myriad of synchronistic variables that sustain us."
—Sandra Bacon

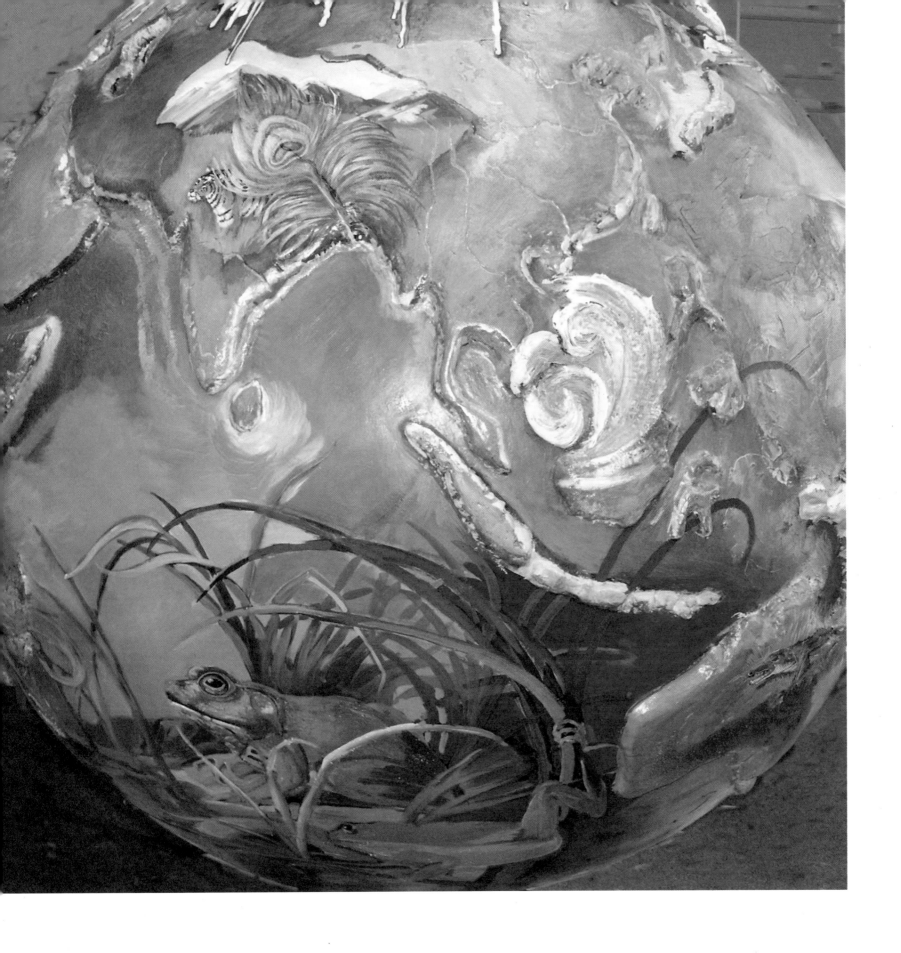

Artists Speak

Green Travel

It is hard to imagine that something as exciting and pleasurable as traveling could have negative effects on the most sacred and untouched areas of the Earth. The concept of ecotourism, a way of traveling by respecting nature, can ensure that future generations also enjoy unspoiled environments around the world. Constance Mallison's globe, a painted collage of thousands of realistic looking landscapes and animals, encourages the conservation of the Earth's precious ecosystems and promotes green travel.

Vote with Your Wallet

Think before you buy. What you buy influences what gets made and that can result in more environmentally friendly products. If consumers want and demand more environmental responsibility from the companies they do business with, new opportunities open up for those companies. There are new technologies to be developed, new processes to be devised and entirely new products and services that can go on the market.

Try to buy things with minimal packaging or recyclable containers. Items made from natural, sustainable or recycled materials. Those with the Green Seal label or the Green-e logo are all better choices for the environment.

Products that are locally produced or grown save the transport cost and the fuel burned to get things from farther away to market.

Consider the effect your purchases have on the planet. Ask yourself how something is made, how long it will last, whether it will save energy and where it will ultimately end up. Use your buying power to help reduce global warming.

"Do you think it's possible to **see it** & do something **about it?**"

Artists Speak
Reuse

Carol Lou Giannasi created an environmentally friendly globe when she crafted it of sustainable materials such as pieces of broken glass, shells and old canvases. The end product is a huge collage that opens your eyes to the many ways household products can be reused before they hit the trashcan.

"Though we make up only **4.5%** of the **world's population** we are responsible for **40%** **of its waste.**"

the three R's

Our capacity to generate waste is shocking and sobering. The United States is the leading trash producer in the world. Though we make up only 4.5% of the world's population, we are responsible for 40% of its waste. In the past 35 years, the amount of trash generated per person has almost doubled.

To stop global warming, Americans need to adopt the "Three Rs:" recycle, reduce and reuse.

Recycle

During the past decade, Americans have embraced recycling and the results have been dramatic. Now we recycle nearly one-third of our waste: paper, cardboard, newspaper, magazines, plastics, glass, aluminum in cans and other forms. The Environmental Protection Agency (EPA) estimates that recycling prevented the release of 49 million metric tons of carbon in 2005.

Buy products that can be recycled or those made from recycled materials. Avoid buying hazardous materials that are difficult to recycle; instead opt for safer non-toxic alternatives for cleaning products.

Artists Speak
Take Simple Steps
Small actions can make a big difference to the environment. The tiny plastic people covering the green globe by Angela Erickson and Chicago's Redmoon Theater represent the members of teeniegreenie.org who have committed their lives to making the world greener by simply changing the little things in life. Turn off the water while you're brushing your teeth, shut down your computer at night, or drive just one mile slower.

Artists Speak
Residential Recycling
Think of what the Earth would look like if we don't recycle. That is the ugly reality depicted on the globe by Faheem Majeed and the Gary Comer Youth Center. The artist and the youngsters worked together and taught one another about the need to reuse overlooked materials found at home.

the three R's

Reduce

Just keeping it simple—buying only what's needed and using all of it—reduces the amount of trash generated. More than 40% of materials entering landfills are paper products. Another 20% is yard waste; 9% is metals; 9% food; 8% glass; and 7% plastic. In 2005, Americans sent to landfills 4 pounds of solid waste per person, per day—more than three quarters of a ton for each person during the year. To remedy this problem, plan meals thoughtfully and compost leftover food. Buy products with little packaging and buy in bulk. Not only does it save money, it reduces waste in packaging.

Reuse

Reusable products preserve scarce natural resources. The average American uses between 300 and 700 plastic shopping bags each year. Twelve million barrels of oil are used to manufacture the billions of plastic bags used annually.

Get into the habit of bringing a tote bag to the grocery store and it could greatly reduce those numbers. When shopping, choose products that are reusable or in refillable packaging. Product packaging generates nearly one-third of our waste. Using other reusable items, such as cloth napkins, washable coffee mugs or water bottles, and even recycled furniture, tools, toys and books are small steps that safeguard the earth.

"I am not a scientist. I am **a mom who cares about the world her children will grow up in.** To protect your children, start with protecting the place they live – EARTH! **You don't need to be a scientist** to implement change. **One simple step is to recycle.**" —JODIE FOSTER, ACTRESS

artists speak

Reduce, Reuse, Recycle

Mitch Levin and Baris Taser reused toy cars donated by children to create their racetrack-inspired globe. After they recycled, they reduced their use of electricity by utilizing pneumatic tools and created their globe's continents from recycled aluminum. Helpful advice is carved onto each flattened piece of aluminum. "Recycling one aluminum can saves enough energy to run a TV or computer for three hours and there is no limit to the amount of times it can be recycled," one of the globe's continents reads.

Artists Speak

Food for Thought

Nicholas Kashian brought the old saying "You are what you eat" to life by shaping his globe in the form of a human head with its parts made up of a vegetarian meal. With the ears as pears, rosy red cheeks as tomatoes, plump carrot lips and pea pod eyebrows, Kashian speaks not only to vegetarians but to meat eaters as well, reminding them that eating just one vegetarian meal a week can better the economy and the environment.

Nearly all of our choices can impact the environment—from the products we use to the food we eat. A new U.N. report states that almost a fifth of global warming emissions come from livestock production. These emissions are due to the large amount of energy required to produce poultry, pork, beef and other meat products. That's more greenhouse gas than is released from all of the world's transportation combined.

You can make a difference with a greener diet. Avoiding meat just once per week can help. It takes far more fossil fuel energy to generate the same amount of protein from a meat source than from a plant source. Try dishes made with beans, grains and vegetables. Choose grass-fed, free-range, organic and locally and sustainably farmed products whenever possible. Eating these foods will improve the planet's health as well as your own.

Artists Speak

Support Organic Products

The portraits splashed upon Vicky Tesmer's globe display a flourishing sustainable farm and a lush growth of nurtured fruits and vegetables. Products from natural farming methods are one way to avoid food grown with petroleum-based fertilizers and damaging pesticides. Today, more than 75 million acres worldwide are farmed organically.

" A U.N. report states that almost **1/5** of **global warming emissions** come from livestock production. "

"The longer we **wait,** the more difficult it will be to mitigate the effects of climate change.

Are we going to **hand our children** a world vastly different from the one that **we now inhabit?"**

—SENATOR JOHN MCCAIN

green home

"If each home in America replaces one light bulb with a compact fluorescent light bulb, we'd save enough energy to light more than

An Energy Star washing machine uses about half the energy and water of a standard washing machine.

3

Dripping faucets waste 2,000 gallons of water a year.

million

homes a year or offset the emissions of 800,000 cars.

Change Your Lightbulbs

Replacing an incandescent bulb with a compact flourescent (CFL) bulb can save $50 or more in electricity costs over its lifetime. CFL bulbs produce only 1/4 as much heat as incandescent bulbs.

98% of U.S. electricity comes from non-renewable sources—coal, natural gas, nuclear power, large hydropower—and 2% comes from clean, renewable resources such as wind, solar, geothermal, small hydro-electric.

the **green** home

"Green Your Home" LUZ MARIA CASTILLO

If you are like the average American, your home could be responsible for twice as much greenhouse gas as your car.

"It's not about everyone doing everything. **It's about everyone doing something**." —ENVIRONMENTAL ACTIVIST LAURIE DAVID

The good news is that you can easily reduce home energy use by targeting energy you lose and don't need to use.

Through proper use of a programmable thermostat you can save about $150 every year in energy costs.

Artists Speak

Water Efficiency

Ginny Sykes's longtime commitment to community activism attracted her to Cool Globes. Sykes is a respected educator, having taught at the School of the Art Institute of Chicago. She used colorful mosaic tiles to illustrate water temperatures and arrows to portray wind currents. Sykes attached faucet handles to the globe representing our ability to regulate and limit water consumption.

Start by choosing energy efficient appliances; selecting the most efficient electrical products can reduce your home energy use by 30% without sacrificing comfort or style. Energy Star is a government-backed program that awards a star to household appliances, electronics and building materials meeting federal energy efficiency standards. If one in 10 American homes used Energy Star appliances, the benefit to the environment would be equivalent to planting 1.7 million acres of trees. High efficiency products also save you money by reducing energy costs.

Another easy way to reduce your household energy use is to replace incandescent lightbulbs with compact fluorescent lights (CFLs) which use one-fourth of the energy and last 10 times longer. If each family replaced five incandescent bulbs in frequently used rooms, it would be like

artists _{speak}...............

Green Communication
Sharka Glet's glossy globe displays two different time periods. Stressing the importance of communication around the world, the top and bottom of her globe encompass the old and new ways people communicate amongst each. Her art suggests that strength in communication can bring on a happy, healthy planet.

taking 8 million cars off the road. In Australia, incandescent bulbs will be phased out by 2010. European Union leaders and officials elsewhere have proposed the same energy-saving measure.

In addition, use lights wisely. Turn them off when you leave a room, and install dimmers, timers and sensors to reduce unneeded lighting. When replacing fixtures, select energy efficient models. Best of all, use less electricity by taking advantage of natural sunlight.

You can also save energy and strengthen your family bonding by turning off the television. Americans use more than $5 billion worth of electricity annually to power TVs. Encourage your family to participate in the community TV Tune Out Weeks, and enjoy non-electronic play, such as board games, cooking, reading, craft projects and sports.

"Energy-based lighting consumes 15% of a household's electricity use. New lighting technologies can reduce lighting energy use by 50% to 75%."

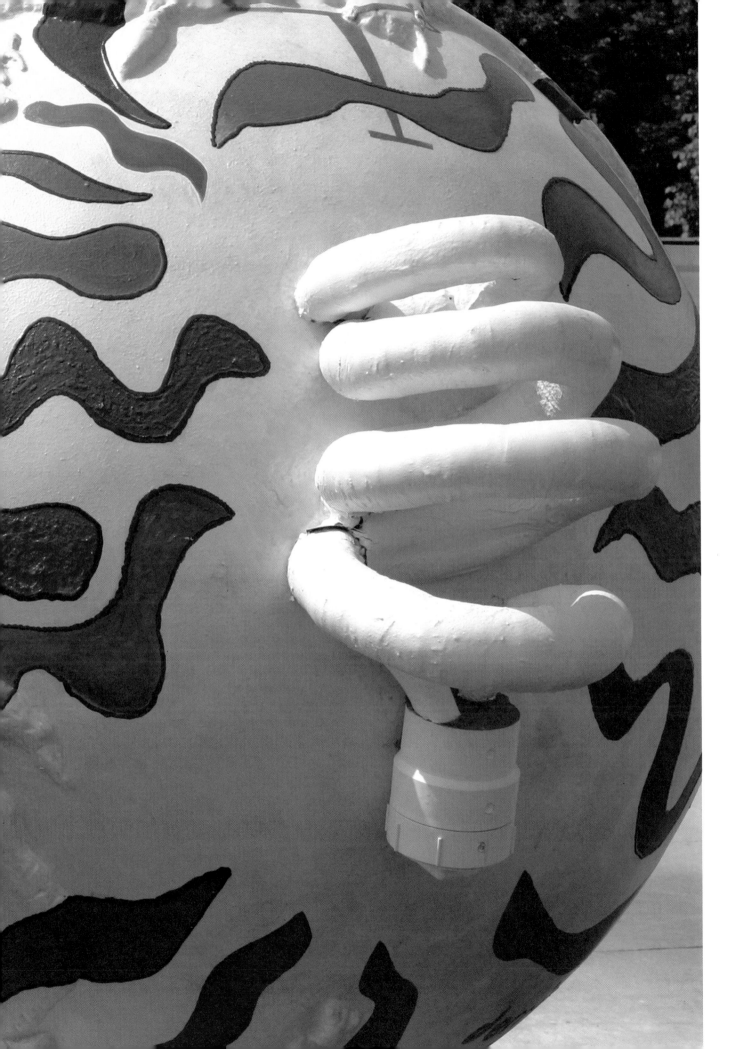

Artists Speak

Change Your Light Bulbs

"The key is replacement of the needed greenery that the earth is being robbed of in order for balance to return. Both land and sea benefit over time, and it takes collaboration and cooperation globally to achieve that."
—Derric Clemmons

stop being part of the problem

start being part of the solution

green home
shopper

Whether you're buying a new home or building one, the decisions you make can dramatically impact both your personal indoor climate and the earth's climate in general.

Paying attention to which way the house faces—or siting the house if you're building—changes everything about the amount of artificial light you need and the climate control indoors. Houses with a southern exposure can use overhangs, awnings or plantings to keep heat out in the summer and let it in during the winter. If you're considering installing solar panels to heat your water, the angle of your roof and how much sunlight you can capture throughout the year are all important.

Those south-facing windows may need thermal drapes and blinds but that will help keep your heating and cooling bills low and reduce how much you need the furnace and air conditioner.

In hot climates, elevating the house—and perhaps avoiding the need for a garage—allows cooling from below. Thick concrete floors and double-glazed windows help moderate temperature changes and keep the house comfortable inside without changing the thermostat.

Warm feet mean a warm body and the thousands of square feet of flooring your home needs have a substantial environmental impact. Manufacturers of environmentally friendly flooring products either use renewable sources or reclaim used wood and make products that help keep a home comfortable. Bamboo and cork are both highly renewable. And cork has the added advantage of maintaining a temperature of 70° degrees year-round.

Reading the labels on building materials and supplies can give you the same sort of critical shopper information as the nutrition label on your groceries. Check for the Cool Roof Rating and a Rediscovered Wood certification. Greenguard certifies paint, insulation and flooring, and the Green Label Plus logo verifies carpets and rugs. Interior paints bearing the Green Seal logo have no or very low levels of volatile organic compounds. The Green Cross logo from Scientific Certification Systems appears on environmentally friendly cleaning products.

If your home can qualify for an Energy Star rating from the EPA, you could qualify for an Energy Efficient Mortgage.

Here are four things to look for when shopping for anything for your home:

1. Environmentally friendly materials—things that are renewable, recycled or reused
2. Low risk to human health and environmental impact
3. Low fossil-fuel or water consumption
4. The potential to recycle or reuse it rather than adding it to the landfill.

Artists Speak

Natural Cooling and Heating

The collaboration between Ross Architecture, Inc., Worn Jerabek Architects and Todd Wiltse resulted in an inspiring look at possible solutions for global warming. With alternative energy options and innovative design methods, homes can be extremely energy efficient. The globe shows some of these methods by using wood screens to create shade and protect buildings from excessive solar heat gain.

Artists Speak

Unplugged Fun

The students and faculty of the Francis W. Parker School used their globe to illustrate alternative ways to have fun. Students between the ages of 4 and 18, included unlimited drawings and endless ideas. The students of the environmental club proposed the idea for the school to get involved in the citywide project and asked others to drop their ideas off before the school went on April recess. After the ideas had been submitted, the school's art director and student design team came up with a plan to bring the ideas to life while at the same time transforming the Cool Globe into a beautiful piece of art.

The children covered the deep blue globe with paintings that inspire others to use minimal electricity and entertain themselves with games like hopscotch and chess. Other detailed drawings include playful suggestions like building sand castles, playing tic-tac-toe, basketball and soccer, jumping rope and selling lemonade.

Make sure when you turn off the TVs, that you also turn off the stand-by power. Televisions and video/DVD players that are off create as much greenhouse gas annually in the U.S. as 2 million cars. Unplug them, or switch off power strips to eliminate phantom electricity use.

Save even more energy by improving heating and cooling efficiency. Seal your home's air leaks with caulking, weatherstripping, or extra insulation. To identify trouble spots, perform a home energy audit yourself or ask whether your utility company offers free audits. Remember to keep vents clean and change furnace filters regularly.

Artists Speak

Adjust the Thermostat

A hand-knit turtleneck sweater, created by Lindsay Obermeyer, is this artist's statement about conserving energy. The large, blue sweater envelops the globe and encourages people to wear an extra layer of clothing instead of turning up the thermostat. Simple actions can make a huge difference and residents can curb greenhouse gases by just adjusting the thermostat.

seal your home

To keep your home as comfortable and climate-friendly as possible:

1. Wrap your old water heater in a jacket designed to insulate it. If your water heater is more than 10 years old, it may not already have sufficient internal insulation. This should save up to 1,000 pounds in CO_2 emissions per year.

2. Caulk and weatherstrip your doors and windows. This should save up to 1,000 pounds in CO_2 emissions per year.

3. Have your utility company do an energy audit to see whether your home is adequately insulated. This could save thousands of pounds in CO_2 emissions per year.

4. Insulate walls and ceilings. You could save 25% in home heating bills and up to 2,000 pounds in CO_2 emissions per year.

5. When it's time to replace windows, install the most energy-saving models. This can save up to 10,000 pounds in CO_2 emissions per year.

You can curb greenhouse gas by simply adjusting your thermostat. Try setting the temperature at 68 degrees in the winter and 78 degrees in the summer. Programmable thermostats let you regulate the temperature to conserve energy when you are asleep or away. Half the energy used in a home is used for heating and cooling systems.

You can also let Mother Nature help with cooling and heating, by putting the sun to work for you. Begin using passive solar energy simply by closing the curtains on hot days and opening them on cold sunny days. Awnings and roof eaves can screen the high summer sun and let low winter rays in to warm your rooms. Vines grown on trellises are an attractive way to reduce solar heat gain during hot months while allowing the sun to shine when the leaves fall off in the wintertime.

Artists Speak
Residential Solar

Legat Architects created a globe with contrasting colors: deep black against light and dark oranges. The light orange represents low energy use while the dark orange shows high energy consumption. Unfortunately for the planet, the dark orange greatly overpowers its lighter counterpart. The globe uses photovoltaic solar panels, which charge by day and serve as power for LED energy lamps during the night.

Artists Speak
Plant a Garden

As a way to display their passion for green solutions, the Douglas Hoerr Landscape Architecture team wrapped their globe with over 2,000 seed packets, inspiring others to green their own environments.

IN THE YARD

Plant a garden and grow your own fruits, vegetables, herbs and flowers, and eliminate the energy required for production, packaging and transportation to the grocery store.

Your yard can also play a role in reducing your carbon emissions. Converting a traditional lawn into prairie is an attractive landscaping solution that significantly reduces household energy consumption; there is no need to mow, irrigate or apply petroleum-based fertilizers. As leaves release oxygen into the air, dense root systems of prairie capture carbon (a phenomenon known as "carbon sequestration") that mitigates global warming.

When organic waste is buried in landfills, it decomposes and creates methane gas. Methane is a greenhouse gas so potent that it traps heat in our atmosphere 20 times more effectively than carbon dioxide. Composting is nature's way of recycling by turning organic garbage into a natural fertilizer for your garden. Insects, fungi, bacteria and water break down the waste in an oxygenated environment, producing no methane gas.

Artists Speak
Composting
Worms, yes worms, live inside Bill Friedman's globe. They speed up the composting process and keep organic waste from going into landfills. Composting is good for your garden and the planet.

Artists Speak
Plant Trees
A larger-than-life pair of hands sprouts from the top of Carlos E. Jimenez's globe. The hands are planting a tree, motivating all of us to help make up for every tree cut down and bring us one step closer to saving our planet.

notes Plant a Tree ....

Every day every person in the world generates an amount of carbon dioxide that requires 10 trees to absorb. Planting trees not only beautifies, it helps neutralize your carbon footprint.

Artists Speak

Conserve Water

Mirjana Ugrinov's talents in painting, fiber art, 3-D installations and set design led her to participate in Cool Globes. She designed her globe to illustrate the importance of water conservation, displaying a variety of water-saving faucets that can be found at your local home improvement store. With the average American family using 350 gallons of water every day, these faucets should adorn the kitchen of every home as their smaller nozzles can drastically cut down the amount of water wasted.

help slow
the flow

Americans can help save energy by using water more efficiently. Water treatment is one of the biggest municipal uses of electricity—requiring power to extract, transport, purify and distribute water. We can reduce our impact by using low-flow faucets, toilets, and showerheads. Quick showers and full dishwasher loads can also save water. Heating water creates even more global warming pollution, with up to 25% of your home energy used to fuel your hot water heater. Set the water heater at 120 degrees or lower to conserve energy.

When doing laundry, make sure to adjust the dial. As much as 90% of the power used by your washing machine heats the water. Use half as much energy just by switching from hot to warm water. By setting the rinse cycle on cold, you use even less energy, and clothes get just as clean.

Your dryer uses more energy than any other home appliance except the refrigerator. Use the dryer's moisture sensor and avoid overdrying. Hang partially dried clothes, or skip the dryer altogether and line dry. When buying a new washer and dryer, choose high efficiency models.

notes CONSERVE WATER INDOORS

1. Dripping faucets can waste 2,000 gallons a year.
2. Leaky toilets waste 200 gallons a day.
3. By checking for leaks and installing efficient water fixtures, households can reduce per capita water use by 35%, saving 5.4 billion gallons of water a day.

Artists Speak

Green Laundry

Thom Cicchelli's globe educates viewers about the energy saving possibilities of such simple everyday tasks as doing the laundry. Minor changes—switching from hot to warm water and hang drying instead of using the dryer—can positively affect the environment. All of the clothes on Cicchelli's globe are recycled thrift store items.

Artists Speak

Green Your Home

Luz Maria Castillo defined her globe by dividing it into colorful boxes, each distinctive area portraying a different solution to global warming. Castillo's unique globe is influenced by a Mexican bingo game, Loteria, implying that we are gambling with our earth.

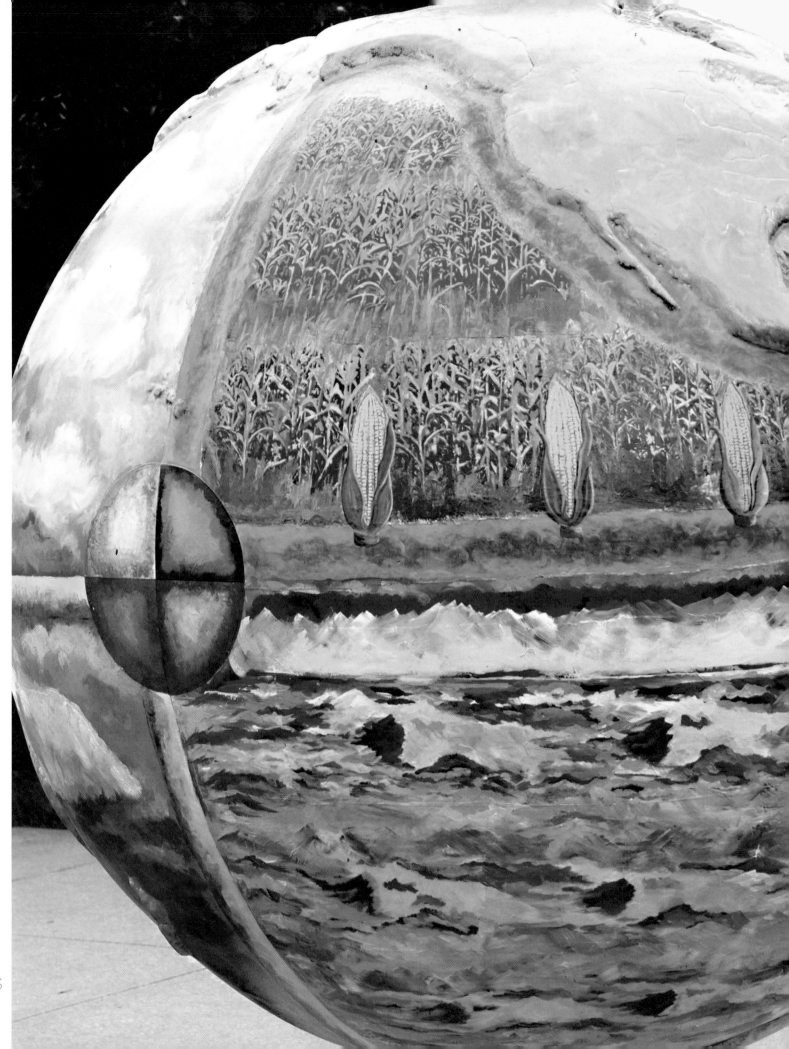

GREEN POWER

Solar technology allows homes to tap into the sun for clean, reliable energy. Currently, more than 10,000 homes are powered by photovoltaic solar electricity in the U.S. If you don't want to install solar, wind or geothermal energy in your home (see chapter 6 for more information on renewable energy options), you can support cleaner energy by purchasing green power. Green power is available nationally through utility companies and the purchase of renewable energy certificates (RECs). RECs cover the additional costs of generating green power and accelerate the development of new renewable energy facilities. For a few dollars per month, you can help add clean, carbon-free electricity to our nation's grids.

"We have the **technology** to make every car **produced** in America today **clean, cheap & efficient."**

—LEONARDO DICAPRIO

going places

"If fuel economy standards increased to

40

Half of U.S. air pollution comes from
emissions from 200 million cars and trucks.

Manufacturing cars with lighter weight steel will also improve fuel efficiency. Industry experts suggest that reducing a car's weight by 10% will reduce its fuel consumption by 2.5%; if a car is driven 12,500 miles a year, 400,000 gallons of fuel will also be saved.

mpg
the U.S. would save more oil than it currently imports from the Persian Gulf. "

"More than 50% of our working population lives within five miles of where they work, and it only makes sense to encourage a healthier, greener generation of people who bike to work. "
—Congressman Earl Blumenauer (D-OR)

Drive Smart

• Keep engine properly tuned
• Make sure tires are properly inflated
• Use a good engine oil
• Use cruise control whenever possible
• Avoid increasing speed while climbing a hill
• Eliminate drag by not carrying items on the roof of the car

going **places** in a **green** world

"Share a Ride" Cheryl Steiger

Modern American society is constantly in motion. More people are traveling further distances on a more frequent basis. Americans travel nearly five million highway miles annually, a 400% increase

in the last half century. Air travel has increased exponentially over the same period. Not surprising, the transportation sector accounts for 30% of greenhouse gas emissions.

A full bus takes the equivalent of 40 cars off the road. The Chicago Transit Authority's newly acquired hybrid buses will produce as little as 10% of the emissions of the standard bus.

Artists Speak

Don't Idle

Turtel Onli created this globe with the help of six students from Kenwood Academy High School where he teaches. He believes all of us are connected through rhythms, styles and practices. Onli's globe illustrates that global warming affects everyone and requires a concerted human effort to stop it.

Fuel efficiency must become a priority in order to reduce carbon emissions. Every gallon of gas a car burns puts 19.6 pounds of carbon dioxide into the air. Increasing fuel efficiency just 5 mpg will eliminate approximately 17 tons of carbon dioxide from the Earth's atmosphere each year.

Hybrid cars take fuel efficiency to an even higher level. Despite the overall car market shrinking by 3%, hybrid sales have risen by more than 50%. Plug-in hybrids are 30% to 50% more fuel efficient than even standard hybrids and get twice the fuel economy of conventional vehicles. Plug-in hybrids have a larger battery that can be recharged by plugging into a standard home outlet.

Considering that half of American cars are driven 25 miles per day or less, plug-in hybrids could eliminate the gasoline used in daily commutes by millions of Americans. The cost of an equivalent "electric gallon" of gas is estimated to be less than a dollar.

Artists Speak

Drive a Fuel-Efficient Car

In the collaborative effort of Lisa and McKelvie Kuppinger, images of hybrid cars circumnavigate this globe. Swinging on metal rods and powered by the wind, these cars score high marks for fuel efficiency but leave no mark on the globe beneath them regardless of how many times they go around.

Artists Speak

Service Your Car

"My approach to this commission came from an appreciation for less complex sensibilities in human existence. The idea is that the past with its primitive systems, its people who lived a simpler life, holds the simple answer to the future's well being and maintenance."

—Derric Clemmons

corporate leadership

Road Warrior . . . .

Toyota's commitment to the environment is not limited to its iconic Prius, the vehicle that has become consumer shorthand for hybrid cars. To date, the company has put seven hybrids on the road.

Toyota's ultimate goal: Improve fuel efficiency and maintain drivability. So far, so good, as the company estimates that as recently as fall 2006 its hybrid drivers had saved more than 178 million gallons of gasoline and prevented at least 1.6 million metric tons of harmful emissions.

Toyota's commitment to reducing waste goes beyond the road, however. The automaker eliminates it on the assembly line as well. In fact, since 1999 the company has reduced the amount of waste it sends to landfills by more than 95% thanks to recycling efforts. What's more, the company has reduced its energy use by 15%, is building new eco-friendly production plants worldwide and even helps its North American dealers manage and reduce service-related waste.

Biodiesel is another alternative for reducing carbon omissions. Made from animal fat or vegetable oil, biodiesel produces up to 75% fewer carbon dioxide emissions than fossil fuels. Not only should we look at what we drive, but how we drive. At speeds above 55 mph, fuel economy drops significantly. By lightening up on the gas pedal and brake, commuters can achieve 35% better gas mileage. Avoid high traffic periods and idling for longer than 10 seconds. Regular tune-ups can increase fuel efficiency by 4%, properly inflated tires raise it by 3%, using recommended motor oil adds a further 2%, and checking and replacing clogged air filters can raise efficiency by up to 10%.

Artists Speak
Illinois
Green Fleets

With an illustration of corn and oil on the globe, Peta Kaplan-Sandzer shows how Illinois is taking a large step in the fight against global warming. Illinois government has become a major buyer of E85, biofuel and flexible-fuel vehicles, acting on Gov. Rod Blagojevich's directive to expand the State's use of cleaner-burning, domestically produced biofuels in its cars and trucks.

Artists Speak

● 1. Choose Alternatives to Fossil Fuels

Peggy Macnamara is currently the artist in residence at the Chicago Field Museum and coauthor of a book on wildlife painting. Her globe, painted with more than 20 types of legumes, nuts, prairie grasses and other vegetation, celebrates the role of biofuels in the search for renewable fuel sources.

● 2. Fly Wisely

Lee Tracy's environmental awareness can be traced back to his youth on the eastern seaboard. "My work responds to our interdependence with our fragile natural environment. My art is both an environmental statement as well as a broader metaphor of our vulnerability and connectedness to the natural order. It acknowledges the co-existence of humanity's destructive and creative energies."

● 3. Drive Smart

Decorated with graffiti-like writing and comic panels, this globe catches the attention of younger audiences. Ian Ray uses simple concepts to illustrate that citizens of all ages can help fight global warming on a personal level.

Artists Speak
Green Vehicles

One of the themes of Joyce Polance's art has been the struggle inherent in both living and non-living things to connect to the world around them. The green vehicles on her globe remind us of the need to examine the connection between the ways we choose to travel and the Earth.

Artists Speak

Use Public Transportation

Sue Sommers uses drawings and wooden frames to decorate this globe with depictions of people riding buses or trains. The human images are arranged on the globe in a way that calls attention to public transportation's ability to bring people together. Sommers shows how public transit fosters a sense of community, in addition to getting cars off the road.

Another way to reduce emissions from vehicles: drive fewer cars. Share a ride. Commuting Americans have so much extra room in our 140 million cars that we could give everyone in Western Europe a ride. If every car carried just one more passenger on its daily commute, 32 million gallons of gasoline and 600 million pounds of carbon dioxide would be saved each day.

Using public transportation is an easy way to cut global warming emissions. A full bus takes the equivalent of 40 cars off the road, a full train can take hundreds. On average, one person commuting by train instead of driving eliminates nearly 5,000 pounds of carbon emissions per year.

Each year, public transportation use in the U.S. saves:

- 1.4 billion gallons of gasoline, representing 4 million gallons of gasoline per day
- The equivalent of 34 supertankers of oil, or a supertanker leaving the Middle East every 11 days
- The equivalent of 140,000 fewer service station tanker trucks
- The equivalent of 300,000 fewer automobile fill-ups each day

Artists Speak

Share a Ride

"We can all make a difference through choices we make in our everyday lives," Cheryl Steiger says, articulating one of the key messages of the Cool Globes project. For this dedication to carpooling, Steiger chose to illustrate the uneven use of automobiles worldwide by concentrating the cars on her globe to reflect the parts of the world that are doing the most driving.

corporate leadership **A Green Fleet** ....

Abbott, the global, broad-based health care company, owns and operates a fleet of more than 6,000 corporate vehicles and each is driven an average of 25,000 miles per year. The resulting mileage, fuel consumption and emissions are nearly double that of employees' personal vehicles, which is precisely why Abbott in July 2007 became the first Fortune 500 company to go "carbon neutral" with its entire U.S. fleet of company sales vehicles.

A typical fleet of 500 vehicles can produce more than 6,000 tons of greenhouse gas emissions every year, according to Abbott, whose much larger fleet represents almost 11% of its total, company-wide emissions. To lower those emissions, the company is not only offering its drivers a new hybrid vehicle option, but will also purchase in early 2008 a series of carbon offsets to neutralize its vehicles' impact on the environment—all in a money-saving effort to improve efficiency, cut fuel use and reduce pollution.

Artists Speak

Ride a Bike
This globe encourages people to improve their health and Earth at the same time by riding a bike to work. An avid biker, Jim Dine wanted a chance to express his love for the environment, cycling and art all at the same time.

Alternatively, try getting around and getting some exercise at the same time. Converting a 20-mile commute to 20 miles of biking each day will save almost 5,000 pounds of global warming pollutants each year. Or walk, run, rollerblade.

As drivers, we often forget that we are actually in charge of what automakers make—how fuel efficient, how environmentally friendly, how forward thinking they are. Drive when you need to but do so responsibly and make your next auto purchase a statement about what you want to happen to the environment.

Artists Speak
Walk

The globe painted by talented artist Eric Stephenson is held up by piles of shoes given to the artist by multiple companies, individuals and celebrity athletes such as All Star basketball player Magic Johnson, Hall of Famer Dave Winfield and members of the Chicago Bulls and Bears. The shoes represent how using one's own feet as transportation can help reverse the negative effects of climate change. Walk for Earth studies show that walking just 30 minutes each day can lengthen your life by more than a year. Instead of driving to work or school, or when running nearby errands, consider leaving your car at home. You'll get some exercise and save some CO_2 emissions.

artists speak ....

Run, Walk and Roll

Walking, running, biking and rollerblading are all eco-friendly alternatives to motorized vehicles. Whether running errands, catching a train or heading to work, try employing one of the methods embodied by the various figures surrounding this globe. Bob Anderson's colorful globe celebrates the daily contributions each of us can make to reduce carbon emissions.

"When I circled the moon and looked back at the Earth. you don't see Las Vegas, Boston or even New York.

You don't see **boundaries or people.**

You know that on Spaceship Earth, there live over **six billion** astronauts, all seeking the same things from life."

—ASTRONAUT JIM LOVELL

urban renewal

" The global population of 6 billion is expected to climb to

Commercial buildings in the United States use 18% of all the energy in the country.

Green roofs can lower a roof's surface temperature by as much as 100 degrees.

billion

by 2020. The global urban population is currently growing at a rate of 180,000 per day. ”

"While cities cover only 0.4% of the Earth's surface, they generate the bulk of the world's carbon emissions, making cities key to alleviating the climate crisis."

Since 1900, the human population has nearly quadrupled while global warming CO_2 emissions have increased 12-fold. The vast majority of population growth will be in urban areas.

NE~~OLE~~

STAR A~~PPLIANCES~~ PUBLIC TR

LY RE~~NE~~WABLE MAT

BON NEU

T FLUORESCENT L

in the **green** city

ENERGY GEN

NATE FOS

WORK RIDE A BIKE

"Translate Words into Action" Stanley Tigerman

FORE

Over half of all heat-trapping greenhouse gas emissions in urban areas come from buildings. In major metropolitan areas—New York and London, for example—this amount can be as high as 70%.

"I see **protecting and enhancing the environment** as part of my life's work."

—RICHARD M. DALEY, MAYOR OF CHICAGO

Green design in new construction and retrofitting existing buildings are necessary and critical steps in reducing the amount of greenhouse gas emissions that contribute to global climate change.

The average urban tree absorbs one ton of greenhouse gas during the first 40 years of its life.

Artists Speak

Eco Students

Using sunflowers as inspiration, The Latin School of Chicago created a design that illustrates how students can take initiative to save the world. The globe depicts how a sunflower can make the air cleaner, along with many suggestions that show individuals how they can help save the environment.

Students submitted approximately 40 possible designs for the globe, and the final project represents a combination of ideas. A stack of books, which serves as the base of the globe, conveys the message that education is the foundation for addressing global warming. Latin's plan of action includes a series of 10 "lessons" which are written on chalkboards circling the globe. The lessons include: ride a bike, carpool, recycle, use less water, take the bus, use less paper, reuse containers, unplug, plant more and walk more. Behind the chalkboards, the globe is covered in sunflowers which the students learned act as natural sponges to pollution in the environment and help purify the air.

artists speak

Chicago's Bike 2015 Plan

Linda Doyle drew on her experience creating children's art to give her globe a fun, family friendly feel to complement a fun, environmentally friendly mode of transportation. She draws attention to the many advantages biking offers as a means of city transport under the new Chicago plan, while still emphasizing the more traditional benefits enjoyed by bikers everywhere.

From the Top Down

Commercial buildings consume an estimated 65% of all electricity. Now many architects and developers are trying to lessen their impact through sustainable building design, creating ecologically sensitive structures that do not deplete natural resources through their construction or use. They use recycled or renewable materials like flooring made of cork scraps or fast-growing bamboo. Builders save water with low-flow faucets and cut fossil fuel use with passive solar heating, photovoltaic roof tiles and energy-efficient applicances.

teach your children

A good educational plan is essential to lay the foundation for behavioral change in response to global warming. Environmental education is too often a peripheral subject in schools, added on to other lessons as an afterthought.

Learning to live differently, acting in response to the threat of global climate change and lowering our carbon emissions are common goals we all need to embrace. In order to learn how to assess and change our ecological footprint, we need to educate.

Good solid information about global warming, woven into the fabric of all facets of school life, is an important goal for educators to pursue. Students learn from more than the curricula. Encouraging people to live more responsibly demands role models.

If educators begin to involve children in lowering the carbon emissions of their schools and link that to their homes, it becomes a community-wide effort.

Help children establish safe routes to school for walking and bicycling. Stop the idling of waiting school buses and carpool vehicles that pour carbon into the atmosphere. Track the full cost of food coming into the cafeteria and track lunch waste and work to find ways to bring it down to zero. Teach children where things come from and where they go. Use both sides of all paper, open the windows to cool classrooms and lift the shades to provide daylight, caulk the windows. Recycle everything possible.

When social values reflect environmental realities a sea change will occur that will lower our collective impact on the planet. Living lightly will become the norm.

—Jayni Chase, founder of The Center for Environmental Education

Artists Speak
Green Schools

By simply using energy more efficiently, schools can help reduce global warming. The Lawrence Hall Youth Service Center collaborated on ideas for its globe including images of green schools, a more energy efficient design for the center and the benefits green schools will receive for taking care of the world. One of the oldest child-welfare agencies in Illinois, Lawrence Hall delivers an essential continuum of care — a lifeline of action, hope and opportunity — that enables children to build more promising futures.

carbon neutrality

3. Translate Words into Action

On Stanley Tigerman's globe red symbolizes the countries that are most responsible for the deterioration of the Earth, due to unsustainable choices. Green symbolizes the countries that have chosen sustainable solutions, and should encourage the "red" countries to implement the green way of life. The bold words on each country are meant to urge them to take action. Tigerman, an architect took on a project that had become a political football in Chicago. He agreed to design the $25 million Leadership in Energy and Environmental Design (LEED)-certified facility for the Pacific Garden Mission, Chicago's oldest homeless shelter. The building, to open in October 2007, will have a greenhouse where vegetables will be grown for the center's kitchen, a 16,000 sq. ft. green roof, solar panels and energy-efficient heating and cooling systems. The mission's residents will also grow herbs for area restaurants.

Artists Speak

1. Population Awareness

The world faces a difficult challenge today with its growing population and increasing CO_2 emissions. Darrin Hallowell uses multi-colored fabricated plastic pills to map out the different populations. Each pill represents a certain population and allows viewers to see the surprisingly large population densities and their effects on our natural resources.

2. Urban Greening

A sculpted Tree of Life dominates this globe from Kim Massey, who hails from South Korea. She calls attention to the need for urban greening, and the role trees play in that endeavor. The importance of trees in maintaining a healthy earth will be evident to anyone who walks by this globe.

4. LED Traffic Lights

Light emitting diodes, or LEDs, use considerably less energy than regular stoplight bulbs. Lee Strickland's globe is powered by an LED solar panel and is decorated with plant and fruit-shaped LED traffic lights to symbolize their Earth-friendly nature. Chicago plans to reduce carbon dioxide emissions by 1.2 million tons annually, by switching to LED stoplights.

5. Commercial Solar

An infinity symbol connecting this globe to the sun conveys in succinct and elegant fashion the sun's vast power, and the Earth's potential to benefit from it. Carlos E. Jimenez, who came to Chicago from Costa Rica at the age of two, further underscored this message by decorating the globe with warm tones and gold material reflecting a world powered by solar panels harnessing energy from our closest star.

6. Rebuild Green Cities

Using the devastation of her hometown—New Orleans—as her inspiration, Karen Perl uses an array of pictures to tell the story of a city left unbroken. Landmarks, voodoo symbols and a healthy-looking Mississippi atop the globe, show that the reconstruction of New Orleans is underway and the city will be even more eco-friendly than before.

7. Commercial Recycling

"I'm a city artist so anything I find in the street, I recycle it and make it into my own artwork," says artist Bryan Sperry whose experience with found-object sculpture was a natural fit for this Cool Globe theme. The globe features found items such as drainage tubes, an old wok and a metal lampshade. "The point is, 'Don't waste stuff,'" says Sperry.

8. Lighting the Future

Light-emitting diodes, compact fluorescent bulbs and other energy-saving advancements in lighting are celebrated on this globe by Peter Mars. Mars has been at the forefront of Chicago's Avant Pop Art movement for the past 15 years. Viewers can learn how using more efficient light bulbs benefits "Ice Bear," Mars' own friendly Pop Art emblem of all that's endangered by global warming.

9. Chicago's Green Leadership

Mayor Richard M. Daley wants to make Chicago "the greenest city in America" and has started to orchestrate programs to realize this ambition. Jonathan Franklin, self-proclaimed "radical conservative," shows his passion for conservation in his globe. The globe features large plants growing near the city's trademark sites, illustrating that the government and citizens of Chicago can make this green dream a reality.

10. Sustainable Building Design

The Chicago-based architectural firm of Nagle, Hartray, Danker, Kagan, McKay and Penney used salvaged brick, glass and concrete diverted from the landfill for its globe. The bench is a roof joist reclaimed from an old barn. NHDKMP invites viewers to "Have a seat by the globe, and remember when you leave that there's an opportunity even in the simplest construction to implement sustainable design."

the energy efficiency building retrofit program

The creation of the Energy Efficiency Building Retrofit Program was formally announced by President Bill Clinton in May 2007 as a project of the Clinton Climate Initiative (CCI). The program brings together the world's 16 largest municipalities—Bangkok, Berlin, Chicago, Houston, Johannesburg, Karachi, London, Melbourne, Mexico City, Mumbai, New York, Rome, São Paulo, Seoul, Tokyo and Toronto—with four of the world's largest energy service providers and five of the world's largest banks to provide cities with the requisite energy audits as well as the necessary funds to retrofit existing buildings at no net cost.

Under the program's arrangement, cities can borrow funds to make proper retrofitting adjustments, and pay back the loans with the energy savings that will immediately be realized. As the first of several programs the CCI is undertaking with the C40 Large Cities Climate Leadership Group, the retrofit program will have a measurable and sustainable impact on reducing global climate change.

The CCI estimates that less than 1% of the potential U.S. market for retrofitting existing buildings is currently being tapped. Retrofit programs are even scarcer in Europe and Japan and hardly exist in the rest of the world at all.

Artists Speak
Urban Forests

The plants and trees that provide shade, remove pollution and reduce traffic noise in cities are known as urban forests. Kate Tully paints four different types of trees, hugging the globe and overlapping the regions of the world from which they originate. The idea is to represent the importance of greenery in urban areas, and to illustrate how necessary trees are to help cool the earth and remove greenhouse gases from the atmosphere.

A green roof collects rainwater, snow and ice and makes parking lots, sidewalks and streets less hazardous. Rooftops made of traditional materials create "urban heat islands," and increase the temperature of cities where large buildings are concentrated. With shingles that redirect UV rays, cool roofs reflect the sun instead of absorbing its heat, lowering a roof's surface temperature by as much as 100 degrees.

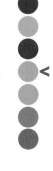

Artists Speak

Clinton Climate Initiative

The Clinton Climate Initiative (CCI) and the world's largest cities have teamed up to fight climate change by offering strategies for cutting greenhouse gas emissions and providing city leaders the opportunity to learn from each other. Artist Sandra Bacon identified the 40 cities participating in the CCI, illustrating the ripple effect they are having around the globe.

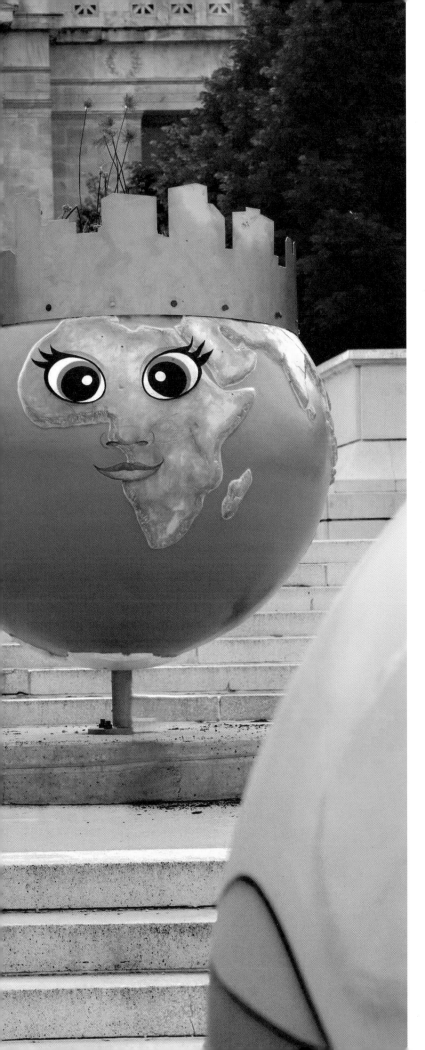

Green roofs help lower the high temperature of regular rooftop surfaces. The greenery in these rooftop gardens helps lower a building's temperature and protect the roof from sun damage. The rooftop garden itself acts as a natural filter for precipitation, absorbing 90% of water and protecting sewer systems from flooding. A green roof not only reduces energy costs and collects precipitation, but also provides an urban oasis for vegetation and animals.

Artists Speak

● 1. Rooftop Gardens Around the World

Rooftop gardens can help protect a world that Ingrid Albrecht has spent much of her life exploring. She taught for four years in Argentina, one year in Costa Rica and one year in the jungles of Guatemala. In addition, she has led numerous travel groups to Botswana, Uganda, Kenya, Tanzania and South Africa.

● 2. Green Roofs Save Energy

Chicago native Deborah Adams Doering used biodegradable coir trays made of coconut, and eco-friendly plants to create the green roof on her globe. It is estimated that $100 million could be saved annually on cooling costs if all Chicago buildings were retrofitted with green roofs.

● 3. City Hall's Green Roof

Mason Dixon currently teaches motion graphics at the School of the Art Institute of Chicago and owns a small media design company, Design After Next. He used cob, an all-natural building material, to construct the representation of City Hall's 33,000-square-foot rooftop garden that sits atop his globe.

● 4. Green Roofs Save Water

"I was excited to be a part of this project because of my personal concern for the environment, a love of nature, a belief in the power of community to advance change," says artist Carol Luc. Students from Evanston Township High School in Evanston, Ill., worked with Luc on the cut steel tiara that represents the Chicago skyline.

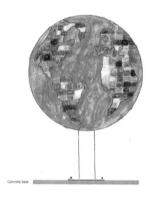

Artists Speak

Cool Urban Roofs

The mosaic shapes covering the continents in Alice Sharie Revelski's globe are made out of energy-efficient roof shingles that reflect UV rays. Reflective roofing materials can reduce the surface temperature of a roof by as much as 100 degrees, mitigating the "heat island" effect created when buildings are clumped together in dense urban areas.

urban
planning

Urban planners are realizing the benefits of shady trees and green spaces, not only as they welcome people to spend time outdoors, but also as they help absorb CO_2. Urban planning can have a significant impact on the city's carbon emissions. Providing paved bike paths, access for bikers on public transportation and free parking gives bikers additional incentives to skip the car and hop on a bike.

  Cities can save money by promoting more efficient energy use in schools. New buildings incorporate solar panels and green roofs. Old schools are changing light bulbs and caulking windows. American K-12 schools could save an estimated $1.5 billion by increasing energy efficiency—enough to hire 30,000 more teachers or buy 40 million new textbooks. Many schools are taking advantage of natural daylight, which has been shown to help student performance go up as energy bills and greenhouse gas emissions go down. Schools are also teaching children by leading by example. Instituting paper recycling programs, waste-free lunches, and encouraging kids to walk or bike to school. At Chicago Public Schools, Conservation Clubs are doing energy audits and waste reduction projects.

Lighting the Future

One of the most environmentally promising developments is how we choose to light our spaces. Compact fluorescent (CFL) bulbs are already a drastic improvement over regular incandescent bulbs in every environmental term. A further improvement is LED (light-emitting diode) bulbs. We tend to think of them as only the indicator lights on our stereos or the numeric displays on digital watches, but LEDs are making their way into office buildings and having a big impact. With a life cycle upwards of 60,000 hours, LED bulbs consume only 1.5 to 10 watts of electricity (1/3 to 1/30th of incandescent or CFL light bulbs).

Artists Speak
LEED Buildings
Farr Associates, the first firm to design two LEED Platinum-rated buildings, has constructed a globe dedicated to the company's goal of creating places that enrich human life while minimizing negative environmental impacts. "We see our work happening at the dynamic intersection of three disciplines: architecture, planning and preservation. Our work is inspired by our mission: designing sustainable environments."

"Our last best **hope** **to stop** climate change **is the** **free market** **itself.**"

—ROBERT F. KENNEDY JR.

corporate initiatives

"Renewable energy industries provide

Among Fortune 100 companies, 60% adopted sustainable practices to strengthen their brands or differentiate products, and more than 50% of companies de-select suppliers for not meeting formal sustainability standards.

1

million

jobs, most of them skilled and well-paying. "

Most of the U.S. workforce uses computers. Laptops are more efficient than desktop models and those bearing the 80 PLUS logo use 25% less energy. Using LCD instead of CRT monitors and enabling power management features also save energy.

Investments in renewable energy hit a record $30 billion in 2006, approximately 20% to 25% of the total investments in the energy industry worldwide.

doing well by doing **good**

"Buy Green-E Products" Angelina Villanueva

Corporate leaders, once thought to be unlikely allies in the fight against climate change, are now leading the charge. Companies are recognizing that they can improve the bottom line by

"When **companies partner** with NGOs (non-governmental organizations) and civil societies, **magical things** can happen."

—BOB LANGERT, VICE PRESIDENT, CORPORATE SOCIAL RESPONSIBILITY, MCDONALD'S CORPORATION

increasing energy efficiency, eliminating waste and meeting the market demand for more environmentally friendly products. In the process, corporations are proving there is "green in being green."

Voters aren't the only voices calling for leadership from elected officials. Businesses and environmental groups have joined forces to form the United States Climate Action Partnership (USCAP). Companies, including Caterpillar Inc., Ford Motor Company and PepsiCo, joined leaders from the Natural Resources Defense Council and Environmental Defense, among others, to request that the federal government implement firm caps on carbon emissions.

Forward-thinking companies and manufacturers are designing products that use fewer raw materials and have better environmental performance. These green products are designed to use less energy, weigh less, minimize packaging and contain fewer or no hazardous substances. They are also meant to last longer and be easy to disassemble so the components can be recycled.

Corporations play a key role, not only in making products "greener" but also in the research and development of new products, particularly within the area of renewable energy and sustainable technologies.

As consumer demand for green products increases, businesses are working harder to earn their loyalty. Some companies are motivated to utilize renewable energy sources to power their manufacturing in order to earn the "Green-e" logo certification. Green-e is the nation's leading independent certification program for renewable energy. Similarly, Energy Star recognizes electronics and appliances that are most energy efficient by labeling products with a seal of approval.

Artists Speak
Green Your Screens
Robert Chamber's strategically colored globe illustrates the impending threat of global warming. Green ranges symbolize areas with environmentally aware populations offering a potential for change while red and yellow show the places that need to speed up their green processes.

artists speak ....

Nanotechnology and the Age of Replication
Penny Feuerstein's participation in the Cool Globe project began with a long-standing desire to use her art as a vehicle to give back to the community. "Little did I know, at the outset, how perfectly my artwork would dovetail with this environmental project," Feuerstein said. Basing her globe around the concept of nanotechnology, a field that many believe will allow for a more eco-friendly world by decreasing waste, saving energy and reducing the need for fossil fuels, Feuerstein found a direct connection between her own artwork and the concepts behind nanotechnology.

corporate leadership

Mohawk Fine Papers is a leading producer of recycled papers, including a line that is made of 100% recycled wood fibers. Mohawk not only saves over 300,000 trees annually, but also meets the Green Seal Certification Standards for use of post-consumer waste.

Mohawk doesn't just recycle paper, though. It also recycles air. Owner of the only wind-powered paper mills in the United States, the company is among the 25 largest purchasers of wind-generated electricity among U.S.-based manufacturing companies.

Mohawk currently purchases 100 million kWh of wind power—enough to generate 100% of the electricity needed to power each of its paper mills in New York and Ohio.

Where recycling and wind energy can't help, Mohawk is reducing its environmental footprint by going "carbon neutral," offsetting its remaining emissions with carbon offsets that will fund emission-free energy projects nationwide.

Artists Speak

● 1. Green Revitalization

Castings of a pine tree and a six-foot-tall mold of a hand is a way for artist Phil Schuster to urge people to want to use every human hand in the fight to save the planet. The inspiration for this piece comes from Schuster's constant involvement in growing exotic conifer seedlings at his studio, and his strong feelings about the importance of evergreen forms in the environment. Schuster is a sculptor with over 25 years experience in creating bas-relief sculptures and public art environments.

● 2. Green Office

Designed by Cathryn Henry-Colcer and Dan Colcer, this globe depicts two cities side-by-side. One has decided to go green, the other to ignore the environment around it. In one city, workers commute by mass transit and recycle—and enjoy blue skies and a clean environment. In the other, every car carries a single person and every factory belches smoke. What you do changes how you live.

● 3. Creative Innovation

The heaviest globe on display, at over a ton, the metal covering the globe weathers with each passing day. The parallel is the impact of human behavior on our real globe, worsening each day without environmental changes. Artists Todd Hoffman, Alfonso "Piloto" Nieves and J. Omar Magana "locked" the globe to represent the shackles of global warming and the search for a key to solve it.

● 4. Green Manufacturing

David Gista, who emmigrated from France seven years ago, illustrates the need to pay attention to where our consumer products come from. He has painted his globe to show the backs of people watching green manufacturing take place. Anyone who sees the globe is invited to do the same: to watch and make sure you are consuming environmentally friendly products.

Artists Speak

Buy Green-E Products

The Green-e logo on certified products and appliances marks a huge step toward saving our natural resources. Angelina Villanueva, who chose to participate in Cool Globes on behalf of her children, empowers viewers to use environmentally friendly energy.

Sustainable

Agribusines

Agriculture contributes approximately 7% of all U.S. greenhouse gas emissions. Opportunities for farmers to reduce energy and greenhouse gas emissions range from rotating crops and improving irrigation to using biodiesel tractors and farming without tilling. By eliminating tilling, carbon dioxide absorbed by plants remains underground instead of being released into the atmosphere. Soil conservation techniques on U.S. cropland could store about 14% of our nation's annual carbon dioxide emissions.

Many corporations are not only working to reduce their own carbon footprints, but they are demanding similar initiatives from their suppliers and vendors, thus setting off a ripple effect throughout industries. McDonald's Corporation created an environmental scorecard for its suppliers in an attempt to encourage energy efficiency throughout its supply chain.

In the United Kingdom, plans were announced to develop a carbon footprint labeling system similar to the way food products are labeled with nutritional content. Products will be labeled with their environmental impact to show consumers the production, transport and disposal impact of products.

corporate leadership Starbucks

In 2001, Starbucks partnered with Conservation International and Scientific Certification Systems to design its sustainable coffee program—Coffee and Farmer Equity (C.A.F.E.) Practices. The program rewards coffee growers who meet a strict set of economic and environmental standards. The prize for growers is preferential buying status, higher prices and more favorable contract terms.

In 2006 alone, Starbucks purchased 53% of its total coffee supply from C.A.F.E. Practices-approved growers, and another 11% from other sustainable suppliers. It bought more than 155 million pounds of environmentally friendly, economically transported coffee beans.

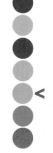

Artists Speak

Sustainable Farming

A colorful array of organic products such as coffee beans, parsley, barley, blue and yellow corn cover every inch of Kari Kaplan's organic-mosaic globe. The produce found in each region of the world helps the viewer understand that crops farmed in a sustainable manner are both helpful to the environment and healthy to consumers. A Starbucks Coffee employee, Kaplan hoped to help the world understand the importance of conserving energy. Kaplan and her mother spent two months hand gluing the hundreds of thousands of grains and seeds.

Artists Speak

Green Investing

In 2006 a record $30 billion was invested in renewable energy. It is great to see major financial institutions investing in green technology and encouraging their clients to do the same. Jessica Pignotti's globe is covered with large flowers and greenery growing from a foundation of paper money. The globe illustrates the need to invest in companies that support sustainable green products and celebrates the idea that a healthy planet is possible when businesses and individuals come together.

Cap and Trade

Under a cap and trade system, a limit is put on total carbon emissions, and then allowances for CO_2 are given or sold to individual companies. Those that reduce emissions quickly can sell their excess allowances to others who exceed their limits. Cap and trade provides companies the flexibility to invest in clean energy solutions to reduce emissions in the most efficient and cost-effective manner possible.

In 2006, the groundbreaking California Global Warming Solutions Act passed, mandating a reduction of CO_2 levels by 25%. To achieve these reductions, Gov. Arnold Schwarzenegger said, **"We want a market-based system to give business incentives."**

Artists Speak
Cap and Trade
An administrative approach used to control pollution by providing economic incentives for achieving reductions in the emissions of pollutants, "cap-and-trade systems" are one way to globally reduce greenhouse gas emissions. This globe is a diagram of the cap-and-trade system, but is within the context of a human heart, illustrating the relationship between economy and health.

artists speak ....

Solar Economics
The solar panels and light-emitting diodes inside this globe help artist Ted Sitting Crow Garner to stress the importance of solar energy. This globe is unique because it uses the alternative form of energy it advocates. By storing solar energy during the day, the globe becomes illuminated at night to display currency symbols from around the world.

Job Creation

All of these corporate initiatives, environmental technologies and research are resulting in a need for employees with new skills. "Green collar" jobs are expanding in the fields of energy and water conservation, alternative energy, waste management, home efficiency, landscape management and food production.

Corporations have come a long way beyond the simple idea of "doing well by doing good." They are reinventing how business is done, creating new jobs and entirely new industries. Becoming part of the solution to climate change is more than enlightened self-interest; it is the new face of global business.

Artists Speak

Work for the World

The equator reads "We the People of the Planet Earth, in Order to form a more perfect Environment, establish ecological Balance, insure sustainable Habits, provide for Intelligent Dialogue, promote the Well-Being of all, and secure the Blessings of the natural World to ourselves, and Posterity, do ordain and establish this promise for Global Responsibility." IIT's globe was designed by College of Architecture professors Catherine Wetzel and Richard Nelson and was created by graduate architecture students John Castro, Katie Hart, Bridget O'Connell, Tyler Waldorf, Andrew Widman and Camille Yu.

artists speak ....

Save Snow

Jaume Plensa, creator of Millennium Park's Crown Fountain, created a black globe that asks two simple questions: "Who?" and "Why?," the questions Albert Einstein asked during World War II.

Ski resorts in the U.S. are working hard to fight global warming and the Save Snow campaign was the basis for Plensa's questions.

Artists Speak

**Research
and Conservation**

Amy Lowry's oil
painting of life-like
large leafy trees
and living species
endangered by
global warming
raises awareness
of a dire need to
stop deforestation.
Although research
has helped to
bring a fuller
understanding
of the beauty
and importance
of maintaining
our natural
landscapes, the
need to create
national parks
and protect
natural areas
across the world is
paramount.

Research and Conservation

Research has helped us more fully understand the beauty and importance of natural treasures. Until a few years ago, Cordillera Azul, Peru, with its magnificent peaks and fog-shrouded forests, remained a mystery to all but a few. A team of experts from The Field Museum conducted a rapid inventory of this remote region, producing powerful documentation that resulted in the Peruvian government's creation of their new 5,213-square-mile national park.

The conservation efforts of The Field Museum have resulted in the safeguarding of more than 35,000 square miles of intact forests. These new protected areas are now safe from biodiversity loss and deforestation. Worldwide, deforestation is throwing hundreds of millions of tons of carbon dioxide into the atmosphere each year. These undisturbed forests soak up the damaging, excess carbon dioxide from the atmosphere.

Did you realize The Field Museum was changing the map of the future?

Artist: Amy Lowry, "Terra Verte"
Sponsor: Marshall Field V

Events We Love and the People Who Plan Them

Artists Speak
Lollapalooza

Lollapalooza, a musical, cultural and community experience, drew 160,000 people to Chicago's Grant Park for three days to listen to 130 bands—and to learn how to lighten their eco-step. The festival focused on taking positive actions to lighten its ecological impact and introduced a new section of the festival, Green Street, which included a patron recycling area, eco-friendly vendors and a city-sponsored pledge drive with five simple steps to green patrons' lives. The festival's greening message helped educate patrons in ways they can "be themselves, changing their life habits just a little bit" to help the environment, according to Lollapalooza organizer, Perry Farrell. Performing artists signed a Lollapalooza Cool Globe.

The Super Bowl, World Cup soccer, the Olympics and other major sporting events are defeating global warming by becoming carbon neutral. Super Bowl XLI compensated for its energy consumption by planting trees and purchasing renewable energy certificates to cover the additional cost of clean power. Organizers donated leftover food, decorations, building materials and sports equipment to non-profits to reduce landfill waste.

The World Cup soccer tournament in Berlin saved more carbon than it created by funding energy sources that do not emit greenhouse gas. Salt Lake City and Turin fully offset carbon emissions at their Winter Olympic Games, and the 2012 London Summer Olympics will be powered in part by a wind turbine. Entertainment events including rock concerts, music festivals, movie productions and the 79th Annual Academy Awards also have been carbon neutral.

Winter sports are in need of the most help environmentally. Snow itself could be a distant memory by 2100. If we don't rectify global warming trends in the next decade, there may be no snow even in the mountains.

corporate leadership
ASPEN/SNOWMASS

Aspen/Snowmass is taking steps now to become the most eco-conscious ski resort with a Save Snow campaign, the snow sport industry's first climate policy. Aspen/Snowmass offsets 100% of its electricity use with wind power and renewable energy certificates. It is also the first winter resort to fuel all of its snowcats with bio-diesel. In addition, the ski area built the industry's two largest onsite renewable projects: the Aspen Highlands solar energy system and the Snowmass micro hydro-electric plant.

Artists Speak

Super Green Events

Romero Britto used the inspiration of many giant sporting events —The Super Bowl, World Cup soccer, and the Olympics—to create his globe, advocating the minimization of the public's carbon footprint. The globe, mirroring Britto's well-known elements of cubism and pop with the use of silver graffiti, bright colors and shapes, showcases these high profile green events to show the public that everyone can help make a difference.

"**Nature** gives you something, **man** **changes nature, and** **that changes** **something** **else.**"

—CHRISTOPHER MILLY, RESEARCH HYDROLOGIST WITH THE U.S. GEOLOGICAL SURVEY

energy, technology, sustainability

"The sun sends enough energy to the Earth to provide more than

10%

Hydro-turbines can convert up to 90% of the available energy into electricity, without producing greenhouse gases or other pollution.

Germany has the most installed wind capacity of any country, generating 20,621 megawatts. The U.S. generates approximately 11,603 megawatts, enough to provide electricity to 3,000 homes.

In the time it takes to snap your fingers, the world uses the energy equivalent of 85,000 gallons of gasoline.

If global temperatures rise 5.4 degrees by 2100, Aspen, Colo., will become as warm as Flagstaff, Ariz., is now.

times the annual global energy consumption.

green technology & energy

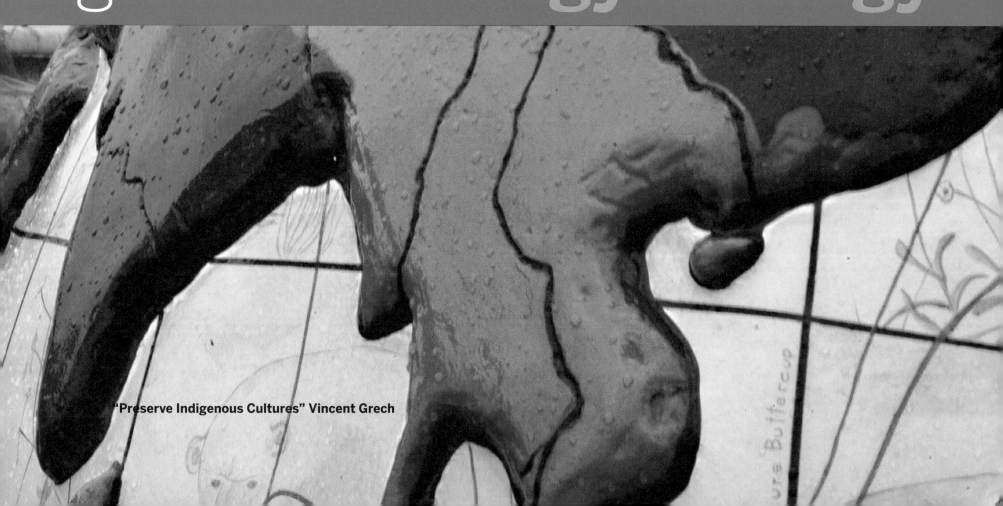

"Preserve Indigenous Cultures" Vincent Grech

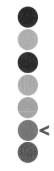

In the U.S., each person uses the energy equivalent of seven gallons of gasoline every day. The United States burns more than 20 million barrels of oil

"**Green** is the new **red, white and blue**."

—TOM FRIEDMAN, AUTHOR OF *THE WORLD IS FLAT*

a day—65% of it imported. Finding alternative sources of energy will not only make us more independent but will improve our environment.

Windy

"A decade from now, there may be thousands of ranchers who will be earning more selling electricity than they do selling cattle." —Lester R. Brown, author of *Wind Energy Demand Booming*

As we search for new sources of energy, we need to look no further than the sun overhead, the earth beneath our feet and the wind all around us.

Geothermal energy can be produced by capturing hot water and steam from deep in the earth or by using the relatively constant temperature of shallow ground to heat and cool. Tapping geothermal energy is an affordable and sustainable solution that will reduce our dependence on fossil fuels. In several Western states, geothermal energy is used to power electrical and industrial plants, while also heating buildings and homes cleanly and inexpensively. Currently, geothermal energy provides approximately 5% of California's electricity. In Iceland, 26% of the country's electricity comes from geothermal sources.

Artists Speak
Renewable Energy
Wind, the sun, green buildings, jungles, hydropower and crops create an Eden on Robert Donley's globe. Donley proposes that by using alternative energy sources, our planet would still be able to operate but would remain untarnished.

artists speak ....

Geothermal Energy
Deirdre Fox is a contemporary artist who integrates icons and unique methods into transcendent artwork that is both art and artifact. For this exhibit, she examines the continuum of life, death and renewal to stress the importance of tapping into geothermal energy sources to reduce fossil-fuel dependency. Beneath the layers of rock, the Earth's surface contains a great many rock springs and geysers that could create an abundance of natural energy.

Hydropower is captured from the movement of tides, the crashing of waves and the channeling or damming of rivers. Harnessing hydropower currently generates about 20% of global electricity. The United States is the second largest producer of hydropower in the world and we use it for 7% of our own electricity needs.

Hydro-turbines can convert up to 90% of the energy from water into electricity, without producing greenhouse gases or other pollution. They prevent the burning of 22 billion gallons of oil annually.

Landfill gas (LFG) is composed of about 50% methane. This natural by-product of decomposing organic matter is a greenhouse gas when released into the atmosphere. LFG, when extracted from landfills using a series of wells and a vacuum system, can be used to produce electricity, as an alternative to fossil fuels, or refined and injected into the natural gas pipeline. Capturing and using LFG is a cost-effective way to turn a harmful greenhouse gas into an alternative source of energy.

Preserve Indigenous Cultures

There are about 370 million indigenous people from 70 different countries whose existence is being threatened by damaged ecosystems. After abundant research, Vincent Grech created his globe to represent the continents from a cultural perspective, highlighting biodiversity hotspots. The background of the globe consists of gridlines and within the gridlines are pictures of endangered plants and animals from throughout the world. Grech hopes that his globe brings awareness to just how delicate our ecosystem really is.

artistsspeak.............

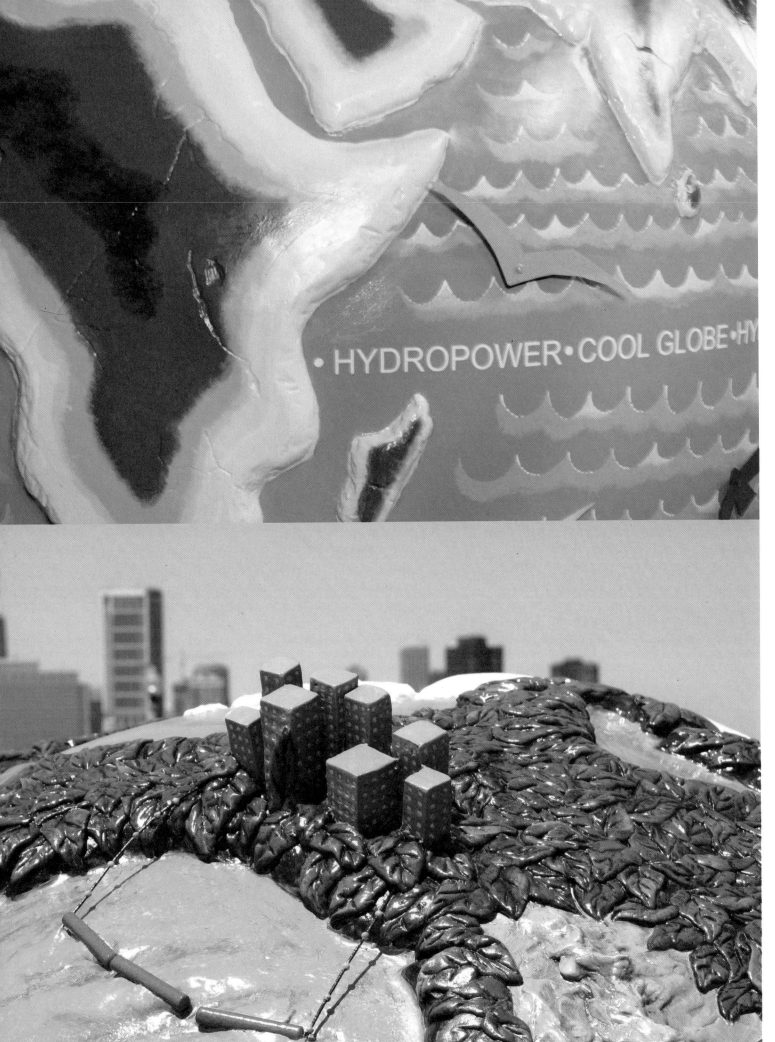

Artists Speak

Hydropower

"Personally, as a Korean of a divided Korea and separated family, I have been longing and praying for peace and reconciliation in the world. It has been my daily life routine to pray for and materialize my vision of national and world peace through art. As a graphic artist, I desire to share this artistic vision with the people of all nations."
                    —Aesop Rhim

Tidal Energy

Ocean waves create a great deal of power and harnessing that power can create natural electricity. "It is about the Palamis Device," says sculptor Vivian Visser, "which is a long floating barrel-like device that creates energy just by bobbing up and down in the waves off the shore of Scotland. It was the only water power device that I could find that has no negative environmental impact."

Artists Speak

Wind Power

Ceramic and vitreous glass tiles envelop this globe in flowing wind. Karen Ami's mosaic globe shows viewers a world awash with wind, constantly moving and readily available as a power source. Ami is the founder and executive director of The Chicago Mosaic School.

Wind has proven to be an increasingly important source of renewable energy and experts believe the United States could get 20% of its electricity from this source of power. For mass use, power companies build "wind farms" with dozens of huge wind turbines in one area. Many farmers are leasing land to utilities for construction of wind farms, while crops continue to grow around the turbines. New technologies are being developed that will store wind power underground so that it can be released when needed.

Artists Speak
Buy Wind Power
Christopher Burke's globe illustrates the relationship between wind energy—the fastest growing source of electricity in the United States—and the global environment. Burke painted a tree growing and flourishing around the planet, its interlocking branches demonstrating the connection between this natural energy and our entire planet.

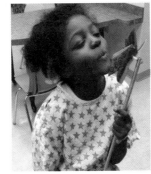

artists speak . . . .

Wind Forms
"During my work over the past five years as a teaching artist, I have been committed to bringing artisitic, educational, and fun projects to the children of Snow City Arts. Participating in Cool Globes was a way to contribute to a cause I am passionate about: global warming and the grave and growing human impact on involving kids of all ages putting their imaginations to use."
—Lisa Fedich

Research and Protect

Research has helped us more fully understand the beauty and importance of natural treasures. Until a few years ago, Cordillera Azul, Peru, with its magnificent peaks and fog-shrouded forests, remained a mystery to all but a few. A team of experts from The Field Museum conducted a rapid inventory of this remote region, producing powerful documentation that resulted in the Peruvian government's creation of a new 5,212-square-mile national park.

Conservation efforts by The Field Museum have resulted in the safeguarding of more than 35,000 square miles of intact forests. These new protected areas are now safe from biodiversity loss and deforestation.

Worldwide, deforestation throws hundreds of millions of tons of carbon dioxide into the atmosphere each year. Left undisturbed, forests soak up damaging, excess carbon dioxide.

Artists Speak

1. Support Scientific Research

The changing climate and its impact on the ecosystems and natural carbon-absorption cycles of plant life, soil and oceans is comprehendible only through science. Naturally, a further understanding of global warming can create an awareness among people to develop ways to solve the Earth's problems. Sharon Bladholm's globe was inspired by her scientific expeditions to the Peruvian and Brazilian Amazon. She based her realistic illustrations on fish collected for study and plants acquired from different botanic gardens around the world.

"My interest in the natural world of the plant kingdom has been a lifelong fascination. I can remember sitting in my grandparents' garden in Chicago as a young child sketching the many types of flowers, vegetables and wild strawberry plants that grew there and from that point have never tired of recapturing the same child-like wonder in creating my works of art," Bladholm says.

2. Protect the Earth We Share

Earth is transformed into a celestial sphere filled with constellations in Compean's work of art. The stars, made out of fiber optic rods, shine at night and the globe contains six stereoscopic viewfinders installed along the celestial equator, where people can look inside the globe. Solar-powered lights illuminate both the stars and the viewfinders, hoping to make people appreciate the only Earth we have. Joe Compean is an eclectic photographer that specializes in photo-documentary. He is a native born Chicagoan and a graduate of Columbia College, where he studied photography. His goal is to provoke communication with and conversation about his subject matter. His work is not only visually stimulating but also thought provoking.

3. Prairie Restoration

Nina Weiss developed her design around the concept of native grasses and their ability to offset the effects of carbon dioxide in the atmosphere and provide a renewable source of biomass that can be turned into energy. Weiss incorporates the textures of nature into her globe by using copper tubing to symbolize native tall grasses.

4. Renewable Energy in Illinois

Chicago artist Alessandra Kelley's globe shows both the benefits and consequences of using different energy sources and illustrates this by using different colors to show good and negative effects on the environment. Blue and green, for instance, represent renewable energy while grays and brown represent ecologically unsound behavior.

Solar energy is abundant, inexhaustible and extremely cost efficient. The sun sends enough energy to the Earth to provide more than 10,000 times the annual global energy consumption. As much energy from sunlight falls on Illinois in 3.5 years as all known recoverable coal beneath it.

Converting solar energy into electricity can be accomplished through photovoltaics, a technology that uses solar cells on panels to capture the sun's rays. Photovoltaics are one of the most promising renewable energy sources in the world.

Solar power is non-polluting, works anywhere the sun is shining, and allows individual users to generate their own power quietly and safely. The solar power market has been growing at 40% annually in recent years.

By using power derived from renewable resources and employing conservation measures, we can displace about 1.2 billion tons of carbon emissions annually by the year 2030. This will put us on track to prevent the most dangerous consequences of climate change. The time for change is now.

Artists Speak

Future Solar

This globe, created by father and daughter William Conger and Sarah McDonald, presents colorful waves representing the solar energy found at the Earth's surface. Nine small white circles spread around the globe to represent solar panels. The reality is that if the panels were strategically placed around the world, they would take up a small portion of the Earth's surface but would collect enough sunlight to meet all world energy needs through the year 2030.

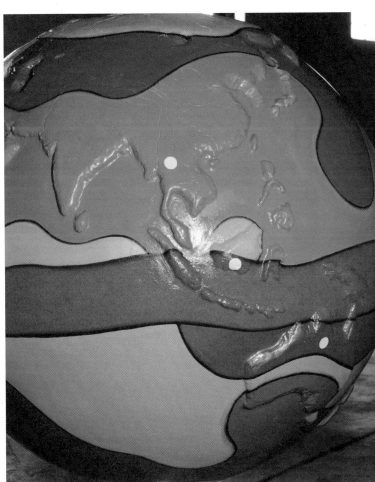

artists speak ....

Photovoltaic Solar Energy

There are many reasons and advantages to using renewable energy sources and photovoltaic panels, as illustrated on the globe by Matt Federico. Mosaic tiles outline the globe in blue, green and brown, and a photovoltaic panel on top of the globe captures the sun's rays, powering the LED lights around the globe and creating a nighttime view of the Earth from above.

Artists Speak

Sustainable Solutions in Developing Nations

Many non-profit organizations have creatively developed ways of using everyday things to harness sustainable resources. Anthony Lewellen featured PlayPumps International and One Laptop Per Child on his colorful globe. Depicting sustainable solutions in developing countries, Lewellen showcases how alternative energy can help those in need, be fun and give the Earth a chance to rejuvenate.

Sustainable Ecosystems

A third of the world's six billion people do not have access to commercial energy. Most live in developing countries, where populations will swell by another two billion by 2020. To further human progress without harming the environment, innovative non-profit organizations are bringing sustainable technologies to developing nations.

- PlayPumps International provides children the fun of spinning a merry-go-round that pumps underground water into storage tanks, supplying clean water for schools and communities.
- One Laptop Per Child uses hand cranks to power affordable laptops in remote areas, opening up a world of learning.
- Freeplay Foundation uses hand cranks to operate radios that bring information to rural residents.
- Sun Oven solar cooking devices prevent cutting down forests for firewood and offer economic opportunities through micro-bakeries.

When ecosystems are damaged, fresh water, food, fiber, natural medicines and shelter begin to vanish. This threatens the existence of indigenous communities, which comprise 370 million people in 70 countries.

Conservation International (CI) works in areas rich in bio-diversity to ensure that natural resources are used without destroying ecosystems and traditional livelihoods. CI spearheaded efforts to protect Madagascar's Makira rainforest. Clearing by burning the forest released vast amounts of carbon dioxide and the resulting deforestation robbed the area of its biodiversity. CI found ways for farmers to use agro-forestry techniques, which provide larger crop-yields without clearing more land. Makira, now safe from deforestation, will save more than 8 million tons of CO_2 over 30 years.

At least 37.5 million acres of rainforests are lost annually. If we can reduce deforestation, which accounts for almost 25% of annual CO_2 emissions worldwide, we can slow climate change and improve lives as well.

Artists Speak

PlayPumps

Nowhere is the connection between a healthy environment and happy children more apparent than in the ingenious design of PlayPumps, pumps that produce clean drinking water using merry-go-rounds. PlayPumps International is raising money to install these creative, sustainable resource solutions throughout sub-Saharan Africa. Chicago Scenic Studios Inc., responsible for the installation of the Cool Globes exhibit, teamed with PlayPumps International to create a globe — complete with merry-go-round and simulated water effect — celebrating this innovative idea.

"Congress must act, and it must act with conviction to **cap emissions** and **modernize** our energy future. **No more play acting.**"

—CARL POPE, EXECUTIVE DIRECTOR, SIERRA CLUB

leadership and vision

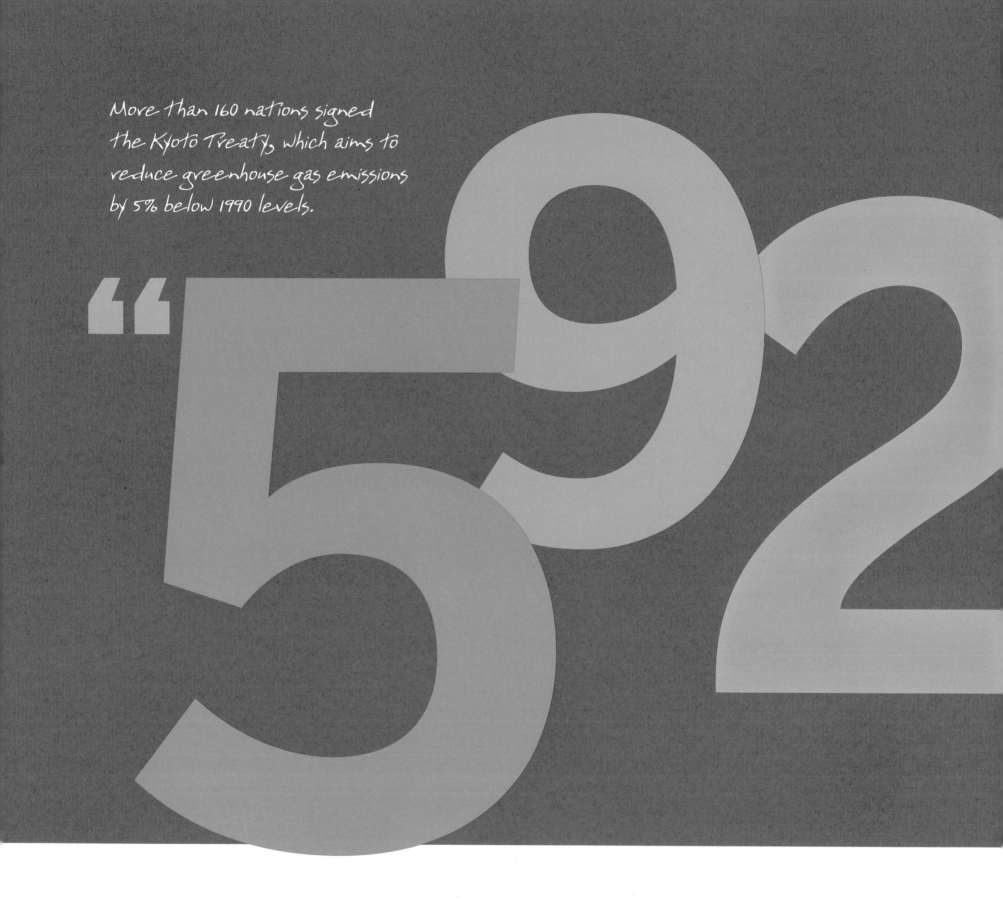

More than 160 nations signed the Kyoto Treaty, which aims to reduce greenhouse gas emissions by 5% below 1990 levels.

"592

"mayors"

have signed the NRDC Climate Agreement.

17 states have committed to mandatory caps on greenhouse gas emissions.

13 states are considering setting mandatory caps.

11 states have set a cap on vehicle emissions.

The Center for American Progress and the Brookings Institution have proposed the creation of an E8—a compact forum of leaders from developed and developing countries who can get personally involved in creating an ecological board of directors.

lead from where you are

"Work Together" RION STASSI AND CITY YEAR VOLUNTEERS

Addressing global warming requires leadership. From government officials to religious leaders, CEOs, celebrities, parents and

"Our **vision with Cool Globes** was to applaud the individuals, corporations and organizations who are **leading the way** in addressing **climate change**. They deserve public recognition—and our hope is that others will be **inspired to follow their lead**." —WENDY ABRAMS, COOL GLOBES FOUNDER

community activists, we all have a role to play. While global warming is not a partisan issue, electing leaders with environmental priorities is critical.

The Regional Greenhouse Gas Initiative (RGGI) is a cooperative effort by seven Northeastern and Mid-Atlantic states to develop a regional strategy for controlling greenhouse gas emissions through the implementation of a multi-state cap-and-trade program with a market-based emissions trading system.

Local, state and national governments can have a dramatic influence on our ability to address climate change. Arguably, implementing a national cap on greenhouse gas emissions at the federal level is the most critical step. Other initiatives include setting efficiency standards for appliances and buildings, requiring higher fuel economy standards, dedicating high-occupancy vehicle traffic lanes and adopting Renewable Portfolio Standards (RPS) which require a percentage of electricity to come from wind, solar or alternative renewable energy sources. Government can also help by ensuring that public buildings are energy efficient, converting public fleets to hybrids, purchasing green power and providing financial incentives for energy conservation via tax credits.

Once in office, elected officials must be held accountable for enacting legislation that addresses climate change. Voters can keep tabs on the voting records of representatives by checking with sources, such as the JAC Education Foundation's voter guide or going to the Library of Congress website (www.loc.gov). Additionally, writing or calling elected officials urging them to vote in an environmentally correct way will remind them that this is an issue of great importance among their constituents.

notes CHAMPIONS FOR CHANGE

In a landmark move, Arnold Schwarzenegger, Governor of California mandated that the California Energy Commission set performance standards for greenhouse gas emissions in the locally owned public electricity sector.

This agreement also coincides with Schwarzenegger's Strategic Growth Plan initiative, which aims to reduce congestion and work toward cleaner air. Among other environmental moves, the governor has signed bills such as the "California Hydrogen

Highway," which allocates $25 million to encourage the use and production of alternative fuels, and the "Million Solar Roofs" plan, which calls for 1 million solar roofs to be built within 10 years.

Artists Speak

Vote for the Environment

Georgan Damore used air brush and fine art techniques to depict patriotic American icons—the American eagle and the flag. Voting for the environment is as patriotic as draping yourself in the flag.

Internationally, our leaders must work together as well. Climate change is a global problem, and carbon knows no bounds. In 2005, more than 160 nations signed the Kyoto Treaty, which aims to reduce greenhouse gas emissions by 5% below 1990 levels. Additionally, international cooperation to share technologies and best practices can play a significant role, particularly with the rapidly rising energy demands of developing nations.

Artists Speak

Global Unity

Krista Babbit used a colorful fabric to outline the countries on her globe that have ratified the Kyoto Agreement. She used black and white stripes to denote which countries are doing nothing to rectify global warming and those that are working together to help stop global warming.

champions
for change

With the following of millions of fans, celebrities can use their fame to shine a light on important issues like climate change. Celebrities in all walks of life—actors, politicians, athletes, rock stars—all stepped forward to create a mini globe in the hope that spreading the word would galvanize action.

Among those who signed mini globes are:

The 2007 Chicago Bulls
The 2007 Chicago White Sox
Tom Brokaw
Hillary Rodham Clinton
Sheryl Crow
Al Franken
Bruce Hornsby
Jim and Jay Lovell
Chris O'Donnell and family
Michelle Obama and family
Nancy Pelosi
Robert Redford
Adam Sandler and family
David Schwimmer
David Winfield
Tiger Woods

Artists Speak

International Cooperation

A large dove with an olive branch in its mouth graces the top of Joe Burlini's globe, symbolizing peace and sitting in front of a rainbow, representing peace after a storm. The globe resembles a diamond, made with laser-engraved Mylar foil that shines and sparkles so much that it can be seen from afar. The importance of peace, international cooperation and treaties meant to achieve a worldwide reduction of global warming is the message of this artist's piece.

Artists Speak

Religious Call to Action

The world encompasses many different religions with many different beliefs, but most believe in being good stewards of the Earth. Deborah Boardman, illustrator and painter, proves with her globe that she believes there is a moral responsibility to care for the environment.

Religious Leadership

As with the Civil Rights movement, the religious community is helping to lead the environmental movement. Religious leaders and interfaith campaigns are pressing for reductions in greenhouse gas emissions, not as a matter of politics, but as a moral responsibility. All religions and faiths share a universal concern to care for and serve one another. *Tikkun olam* is a Hebrew directive to "repair the world."

The Iroquois nation is guided by the principle: **"In our every deliberation we must consider the impact of our decisions on the next seven generations."**

Faith in Place is a Chicago organization that provides the tools to become good stewards of the Earth—from organic communion bread, to solar and lighting retrofits in places of worship, to teaching conservation practices as a matter of faith.

Artists Speak

Heal the World

Tamar Hirschl focuses on the impact that human civilizations have on the natural world. The globe is divided into three parts, each illustrating a potential outcome of human choices. One section shows the Earth normally, another new life thriving amid the creative uses of renewable resources and finally, a scene depicting what would happen if we continue living the way we do today—endangered animals and dying plants.

artists speak..

Seventh Generation

Every culture around the world has differing views regarding their responsibility to the Earth. Beth Shadur's globe features an array of icons including the Iroquois nation's turtle, who they believe is responsible for caring for the Earth; the Jaan bee, signifying the give-and-take cycle of life; and the image of a blackbird holding a white feather, symbolizing ecology. The images and ideas on this globe press cultures to take responsibility for protecting the environment for future generations and to learn from other cultures.

Artists Speak

● 1. Common Ground

Combining objects with images from popular media, Peter Mars' avant pop style tells a tale. This globe, specifically, tells the story of the creatures most affected by global warming — polar bears — taking a trip to the U.S. Capitol to convince political leaders to help stop the rapidly depleting polar ice they call their home.

● 2. Unite to Solve Problems

The globe's phrase: "The well-being of mankind, its peace and security, are unattainable unless and until its UNITY is firmly established."

Sponsored by 13 Cool Globes committee members, this globe is proof that a little collaboration goes a long way. Michelle Maynerick used a background of a bright orange and stenciled intricate portraits around the globe to indicate that what might be overwhelming to an individual is possible when we come together.

● 3. Be a Volunteer

The Chicago Conservation Corps (C3) member Carla Winterbottom used paint and photo collages to connect the world's past, present and future challenges and balances. Echoing

C3's mission to support volunteers in environmentally based service projects, this globe urges people to take action to help maintain a beautiful world.

● 4. Communicate

Vance Williams' globe encourages individuals to spread the word about global warming. The more people are aware of what is happening to our world, the more they will try to stop it. Communication is key to educate the public about global warming and encouraging people from around the world to act.

Get Involved

Grassroots organizations invite individuals to get involved and work on the parts of the issue they feel most passionate about. There are many opportunities to volunteer with local environmental groups. The Chicago Conservation Corps (C3), for instance, trains volunteers to work on conserving water, cleaner air, land restoration and energy conservation. Organizing "Green Your Office" workshops and distributing energy-efficient light bulbs are among the ways C3 supports the city's goal to go green.

"Never doubt that a **small group** of individuals can **change the world.** Indeed, it is the **only thing** that ever has."
—MARGARET MEAD

artists speak ....

Encourage Green Government

Wooden pegs completely cover the globe of Rion Stassi and the City Year volunteers in order to illustrate the intemperate planet on which we live. Reversing global warming is a collective responsibility just as Stassi needed help in creating the globe. It took 10 people 2,800 hours to place the pegs. From afar, the globe appears hot and red but as it is approached becomes blue and green. The inspiration provided by this design is that even small acts can create something world changing.

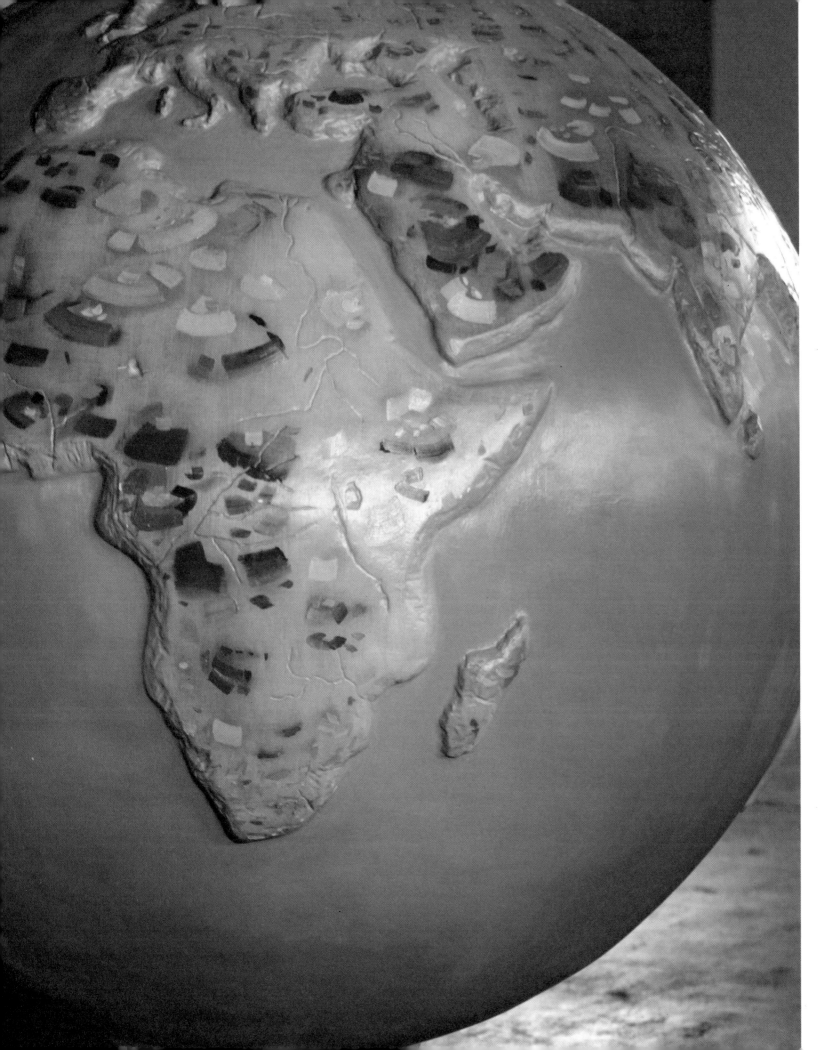

Artists Speak
Care for the Earth
Suzanne Caporael investigates the physical world and transforms the intellectual and methodical data she has collected into sublime and resonate images. Her landscapes often deal with the struggle between man and nature.

Artists Speak

Get Involved

Nancy Steinmeyer's globe reinvents Edvard Munch's famous painting, "The Scream", signifying the Earth's desperate call for help from the terrifying effects of global warming. On the opposite side, Steinmeyer painted Uncle Sam's "I want you" image, provoking spectators to get involved and act within the community to make a difference. "Each of us needs to learn and understand what we can do to help conserve energy," Steinmeyer says. "The actions of each person matter."

Consider getting involved with rainforest preservation to help protect a precious natural resource that absorbs CO_2 and prevents global warming. Or work closer to home, planting trees, tending to plants and preserving nature parks. Find out about your community's recycling efforts. Get involved in reducing the environmental impact of your workplace, your children's school, your place of worship.

The website StopGlobalWarming.org was created by activist Laurie David to mobilize individuals with environmental concerns, and the virtual march—872,000 people and counting—has been joined by celebrities, politicians and corporations lending their support. The website suggests many ways individuals can affect change right from their homes.

Artists Speak
Be Inspired
The modern design of the globe by Adrian Smith and Gordan Gill Architecture features words of different colors and sizes that, when touched by the human hand, can be seen. The words, that are revealed when the outer layer of thermo-chromic paint disappears, advocate the importance of sustainable design and symbolize the power that individuals around the world have to change the planet.

notes STOP GLOBAL WARMING.ORG

Laurie David produced Vice President Al Gore's Oscar-winning documentary, An Inconvenient Truth. She also wrote Stop Global Warming: The Solution Is You. And she oversees the activist website www.stopglobalwarming.org.

Sculptor and painter Tom Van Sant segued from a career of creating public works of art into founding Eyes on Earth, a non-profit focused on environmental issues. In addition to the globe they created together, Van Sant is the creator of the Geosphere, a 24-foot electronically controlled replica of the Earth.

Young Voices

The movement against global warming is mobilizing today's high school and college students. Youth activists are rallying to eliminate carbon emissions at their schools and to influence legislators to clean up America's energy policy.

Groups on nearly 600 American and Canadian campuses have joined the Campus Climate Challenge, aimed at bringing sustainable energy to their schools.

Young environmentalists are demanding action through demonstrations, blogs, online videos and meetings with administrators and legislators. In Vermont, Middlebury College students persuaded trustees to invest $11 million in a power plant fueled by wood chips. Students at the University of California, Santa Cruz voted to pay a fee to buy 100% renewable energy.

Campuses are going green, and students want you to follow. With all ages doing their part to better the environment, a bright future lies ahead.

"The environment is the most important, the most fundamental civil rights issue."

—ROBERT F. KENNEDY JR.

Artists Speak

Act on the Evidence

What appears to be a typical globe from far away—with the usual light blue ocean and green continents—is really not so typical. Eyes, nose and smiling mouth can be seen when closer to one side of the globe. The other side is a not-so-happy scene, with a message of despair in a world suffering from neglect and indifference. Lois Collins' design gives the audience a choice— live in a world of happiness where human action thrives or a world of indifference that will fall apart.

Artists Speak

Student Eco-Movement

Environmental advocacy groups have had a positive impact on the world. Generation Y student activists from around the world are portrayed in a digital collage of images in Thaddeus Tazioli's design. The goal of this colorful globe with realistic descriptions of past and present events is to show that people of all ages can help make a difference.

Empowering Youth

In Kenya, Wangari Maathai, Founder of the Green Belt Movement, inspired and empowered women to improve their lives and livelihoods by restoring the environment through planting trees. The Green Belt Movement has planted more than 30 million trees and recently announced a goal to plant a billion trees. In 2004, Wangari Maathai's leadership was recognized, as she was the first African woman awarded the Nobel Peace Prize.

"Through the **Green Belt Movement** we have helped **young people get involved** in environmental activities. We have tried to instill in them the idea that **protecting the environment** is not just a pleasure but **also a duty**."

—WANGARI MAATHAI, NOBEL PEACE PRIZE WINNER 2004

artists_{speak}

Eco-Heroes

The focus on humanitarian efforts and successes that have been linked to positive changes around the world are featured on Andrea Harris' globe. Portraits of citizens who have helped the environment and relief-form paintings of forests pop up in locations around the globe where they have made an impact. The message is that humans play a large role in preserving forests and planting new trees to help heal the Earth.

Artists Speak

Encourage Green Government

Bernard Williams' globe raises awareness about packaging on products and the things we throw away. The globe, made of recycled materials, also shows the diversity among cultures and beliefs — a cause for local, state, and national governments as they encourage community members to work together for the environment.

Give Me Five

"We can't blow people's minds with our show if all of the seats in our theaters are under water! Global warming is a topic that crosses all boundaries. No matter where you live in the world, or what your political affiliation, global warming is a phenomenon that will affect you, your family, and your community... We need to band together to try to do something about it!"
—Blue Man Group

Artists Speak

Paula Clayton, from New Zealand, loves surfaces. Her work appears on murals and surfaces of all kinds. Her work for Cool Globes recreated the fragile artworks submitted by children from around the world with ideas on how to solve global warming.

Parents can help by giving children an appreciation for the environment. Instead of just reading about faraway rainforests and endangered species, go out together and experience nature's wonders firsthand. Until kids love and connect with nature on a personal level, they aren't motivated to protect it. Skip rocks on a lake and picnic in a park. Go camping. Hike in the Grand Canyon or walk in the local forest preserve. Help children feel comfortable in the natural world before you ask them to heal it.

artists_{speak}

Raise Future Environmentalists

The future of the Earth and the future of our children both depend on how one interacts with the other. Nancy Pochis Bank's globe mirrors an urban street style in order to connect with city families. Being a parent herself, she knows the challenge of getting city kids to connect with nature. This artist wanted to encourage families to become immersed in nature and enjoy the outdoors together. Children who have a bond with the natural world will be more likely to protect it as adult citizens and voters.

LOOK FOR INSECTS
EXPLORE ANY PATCH OF WILDERNESS.
KIDS WHO
THE EARTH
TO PROTECT

"We need to **solve the climate crisis**. It is not a political issue, **it's a moral issue**. We have everything we need to get started, with the possible exception of **the will to act**, that's a renewable resource. **Let's renew it**."

—VICE PRESIDENT AL GORE

Listen to Our Children

At the age of only 12, Emily Abrams wanted her globe to illustrate that even children can make a positive impact when it comes to stopping global warming.

When Emily sent an email asking for submissions, responses flooded in from around the world. The children's answers were common-sense solutions—solar energy, ride your bike, turn lights off. Children see no bureaucratic impediment to solving climate change.

They understand the urgency and they understand that this is a solvable problem. In essence, they're confused by what's taking so long.

Along with professional artist Michelle Korte Leccia, Emily took some of the materials children sent in and covered her globe with them. The resulting collage includes art and ideas from over 25 countries. One—a painting on paper made from Costa Rican banana leaves—urges people to protect the rainforest.

The contributing artists may be young but they are wise. Global warming is a solvable problem and one that must be solved by our generation in anticipation of a better world for our children.

acknowledgements

To the coolest group of individuals I've ever had the privilege of working with—your efforts were truly inspiring—and a reminder that anything is possible when people come together for a cause that is larger than us all. (As Cathy Stein would say, "It's not nothing.")

Thank you to John McCarter and Sadhu Johnston for believing in the vision, when it was just a vision. To John Woldenberg for helping to craft the vision. Thank you to De Gray, who when warned early on, "Don't let Cool Globes consume your life," happily responded, "Too late!" To De, Anne Loucks and Lisa Fremont for finding the most spectacular artists. To Cathy Stein for taking on the heavy lifting, and doing it with a much appreciated sense of humor. Thank you to Lynn Harris, who created a website that even her son approved of—and who worked with me, giddy into the wee hours of the night writing this book. To Nancy Bank, who unlike most of us, was blessed with both an exceptional right brain AND left brain. To Shelly Keilar, who had no idea what she was getting into during that innocent conversation watching pee-wee basketball, but gave it 124%, even on Valentine's day. To Billy Abrams, thank goodness you said yes. Thanks to Lucy Moog, the ultimate team player. Thank you to Jimmy for being the Cool Globes psychiatrist—and for putting up with the insanity. To Karen Segal, for the "gift" of the gala, and Donna Goodman, Gwen Solberg for the perfection in the details. To Jennie Schott, thank goodness your medical training prepared you to work hard without sleep. To Amy Krouse Rosenthal, for making everything sound, look and feel better. To Megan—you're a godsend! Thanks to Karen Frey for a tremendous undertaking in putting together the Business Leaders Roundtable, and for making it look effortless. Thank you to Dipak Jain and the Kellogg Graduate School of Management for hosting the conference. To Carl Pope and Peter Lehner for being part of the panel discussions, and to both NRDC and Sierra Club for going above and beyond with your support of Cool Globes by serving as sponsors.

Bob Kallen, Yumi Ross, Keithe Hayes, Josie Elbert and George Chipain for creating a curriculum that will touch the minds of thousands. To Amanda, the powerhouse of an entire research department, for your wealth of knowledge. To Karen Shoshana, the queen of media coverage. Thanks to Nancy Kuppersmith, Suzy Heller, Linda Ginsburg, Linda Warren and Geena Zaslavsky—commonly known as "the cool girls." Kathy Goldberg, Joe Reinstein, Beth Kohl, Nancy Kohn, Eric Hanig, David Rosen, Rich Coplan and Gerri Kahnweiler for taking on whatever came your way. To Sarah Warren and Carol Oken for being anything but neutral in making this a carbon neutral event. Thank you to Nora Gainer for making the mini-globes a huge success. And to Lori Bucciero—our Camp Cool Globes Concierge. Thank you to Howard Garoon for your gracious hospitality. To Matt Binns, for making it "a better world". To Tom McCormick, Jill Riddell, Laura Coplan, Jay Dandy, Derric Clemmons and the rest of the art committee, for weeding through hundreds of proposals and selecting true talent. To Beth Aldrich and Daisy Simmons, for guiding the guidebook. And to Carla Young, Terry Foster, Cathy Ross, Loree Sandler, Rachel Stern, Wendy Kaufman, Sue Feinberg and Eli Bush for finding the words fit for print. To Jayni Chase, a kindred spirit, thanks for contributing to the book, and for whatever lies ahead. To Nancy Mills, for handling the "cool stuff." To David Heller for giving us Marcelo Halpern and Zak Judd who gave me a renewed respect for the legal profession. To Doug and Christine Belgrad for your star power. To Mike Ellis and the drivers at EA Logistics who generously donated their services, and continued to do so as the project grew... and grew. Thanks to Jim Krantz, Richard Shay and Steve Meyer for pictures worth a thousand words. I sing the praises of Nick Gage for his fabulous song. Thank you to Jung and Nelson for letting us ring the bell—and I'm sorry the market fell.

To the impressive staff at Jasculca Terman: Rick Jasculca, Jim Terman, Holly Barteki, Jennifer Hutchinson, Jessica Thunberg, Marci May—for never missing a beat (no pun intended.) To JAM Productions team—DonnaSue, Matt and Demian—for giving us your all. To Celtic Marketing and EnergyBBDO for your creative energy. To Sheila Cawley and Andrea Powers and the staff at The Field Museum who do so much more than care for dinosaurs and mummies. To Lois Mills, Lynn Goldman, Ali Wein and their outstanding group of docents. To Chicago Scenic for a great job with logistics, and special thanks for creating the PlayPumps globe which you knew would be one of my favorites! Thanks to George Elder and his crew at Luminair for documenting this endeavor. Thank you to Tom Dempsey and Mark Spencer for making the Sears Tower exhibit shine. To Blue Man Group, thanks for turning blue into green. Thank you to Perry Farrell for having Lollapallooza—and all of your artists—join in the fun.

Thank you to Karen Hobbs and Joyce Coffee at the Department of Environment—you were a pleasure to work with from day one. Thanks to the Tim Mitchell and the Chicago Park District, and to Lois Weisberg, Nathan Mason and the Department of Cultural Affairs for your support. Thank you to Sotheby's and Google for making the Cool Globes auction a success.

Thank you to Eric Nonacs for your friendship and for inviting me to CGI. To Sara Richlin and John Needham for your wonderful support of this project. Thank you to Yvonne Acosta, it has been an honor to have Cool Globes mini-globes exhibited at the United Nations.

Thank you to Jim Meyers, Rebecca Rolfes, Doug Kelly, Traci Gregorski, Joline Rivera and their amazing team at Imagination Publishing—for all of your help with this book, and making it such an enjoyable process. Thanks to David Weinberg for your beautiful photography and generosity.

special THANKS

Special thanks to Jim Dine for joining the team first, and for giving us your "heart" and soul. Thanks to Laurie David for being a mentor—and friend. To John Podesta for sharing your genius, and going to great lengths to get here. To Robert F. Kennedy, Jr., a man who can move mountains with the sheer force of an inspiring speech (and thank you for spending your days ensuring that the mountaintops are not moved). Thanks to Al Franken for hosting the auction—your intelligence and wit are only surpassed by your skill for drawing all 50 states freehand. Thank you to Mayor Daley not only for your enthusiastic support of Cool Globes, but for your leadership in addressing global warming. Thank you to President Clinton, it has been an honor and privilege to participate at the Clinton Global Initiative. Thank you for inspiring so many to do so much more.

COOL GLOBES EXECUTIVE COMMITTEE

Bill Abrams
Jim Abrams
Beth Aldrich
Allison Augustyn
Nancy Banks
Christine Belgrad
Sharon Lederman Burack
Clare Butterfield
Jung Chai
Derric Clemmons
Laura Coplan
Rich Coplan
Jay Dandy
Sue Feinberg
Beth Kohl Feinerman
Terri Foster
Lisa Fremont*
Karen Frey*
Linda Ginsburg
De Gray*
Kathy Goldberg
Donna Goodman
David Greenberg
Marcelo Halpern
Eric Hanig
Amanda Hanley*
Lynn Harris*
Keithe Hayes
Andrea Heiman
David Heller
Susan Heller
Zak Judd
Gerri Kahnweiler
Robert Kallen*
Wendy Kaufman
Shelly Kielar*
Nancy Kohn
Jim Krantz
Susan Krantz
Nancy Kuppersmith*
Anne Loucks*
Jessica Lundevall
Tom McCormick

Lois Mills*
Nancy Mills
Lucy Moog*
Elaine Moss
Carol Oken
Maureen Pskowski
Andrea Powers
Joe Reinstein
Jill Riddell
Arnie Rissman
Amy Krouse Rosenthal
Cathy Ross
Yumi Ross
Michelle Sakayan
Loree Sandler
Jennie Schott
Cindy Schwartz
Karen Segal
Karen Bernstein Shoshana
George Spathis
Gwen Solberg
Cathy Stein*
Chuck Thurow
Linda Warren
Sarah Warren
Michael Wilkinson
John Woldenberg*
Carla Young
Shirley Wesse Young
Geena Zaslavsky
*Committee Chairs

ADVISORY BOARD

Wendy Abrams
Founder & Chairwoman
Cool Globes

Jerry Adelmann
Executive Director
Openlands Project

Ted A. Beattie
President & CEO
The Shedd Aquarium

Frances Beinecke
President, National
Resources Defense
Council

Doug Belgrad
President of Production
Columbia Pictures

John Bryan
Chairman, Millennium
Park Inc.

John A Canning Jr.
Chairman & CEO
Madison Dearborn
Partners LLC

Nelson Chai
Chief Financial Officer
NYSE Group Inc.

Paula Crown
Henry Crown &
Company

James Cuno
President & Director
The Art Institute of
Chicago

William Daley
Chairman of the
Midwest
JP Morgan Chase

Laurie David
Producer, An
Inconvenient Truth

Hon. Dick Durbin
U.S. Senator

Marshall Field
Chairman, The Field
Corporation

Jack Greenberg
Former CEO
McDonald's Corporation

Christie Hefner
Chairman & CEO
Playboy Enterprises Inc.

Dipak Jain
Dean, Kellogg Graduate
School of Management

Sadhu Johnston
Commissioner, City of
Chicago, Department of
Environment

Paul H.
Knappenberger Jr.
President, The Adler
Planetarium

Kevin Knobloch
President, Union of
Concerned Scientists

Fred Krupp
President
Environmental Defense

Howard Learner
Executive Director
Environmental Law and
Policy Center

John McCarter
President, The Field
Museum

Randall Mehrberg
EVP, Chief
Administrative Officer
And Chief Legal Officer
Exelon

Hon. Barack Obama
U.S. Senator

Michael Oppenheimer
Prof. Geosciences
Princeton University

John Podesta
President, Center for
American Progress

Carl Pope
Executive Director, The
Sierra Club

J.B. Pritzker
Managing Partner, The
Pritzker Group

COOL GLOBES EXHIBIT
Megan Scarsella,
Project Manager
Lori Bucciero,
Artist Coordinator
Nora Gainer,
Mini-Globe Coordinator

EDITORIAL

Cool Globes
Nancy Bank
Eli Bush
Jayni Chase
Lynn Harris
Lucy Moog
Amy Krouse Rosenthal
Loree Sandler
Cathy Stein
Rachel Stern

Imagination
Rebecca Rolfes, Editorial Director
Beverly Cook, Director of Operations
Judy Crown
Erin Dorr
Ross Foti
Brigette Gaucher
Adam Istas
Kelly Kane
Janet Liao
John Mulligan
Chuck Paustian
Sara Sandock
Erin Slater
Olivia Watkins

DESIGN
Doug Kelly, Design Director
Traci Gregorski, Senior Art Director
Joline Rivera, Art Director
Nicole Cammarata, Designer

PHOTOGRAPHY
Wendy Abrams
Jim Krantz
Bill Parish
David Weinberg

Special thanks to our major sponsors:

Abbott

PepsiCo

Exelon Corp.

Starbucks Coffee Co.

Global Hyatt

Toyota

McDonalds Corp.

Whole Foods

Medline Industries Inc.

We'd like to acknowledge the following for their generous support of Cool Globes ·······························

Adler Planetarium
Basic Wire & Cable
Chicago Climate Exchange
Chicago Children's Museum
Chicago Department of Environment
Chicago Park District
Chicago Scenic Studios
Chicago Sun-Times
Chicago Transit Authority
EA Logistics
Energy BBDO

FedEx
The Field Museum
For Her Information Media
Google
Green Exchange
Hayes Properties
JCDecaux
Jam Productions LTD
Jasculca-Terman and Associates Inc.
The Joyce Foundation
Kohl Chidren's Museum

Kellogg Graduate School of Management
King College Prep
Latham & Watkins LLP
Luminair Film Productions, Inc.
NBC 5
Patrick BMW
Sears Tower
The Shedd Aquarium
Sotheby's

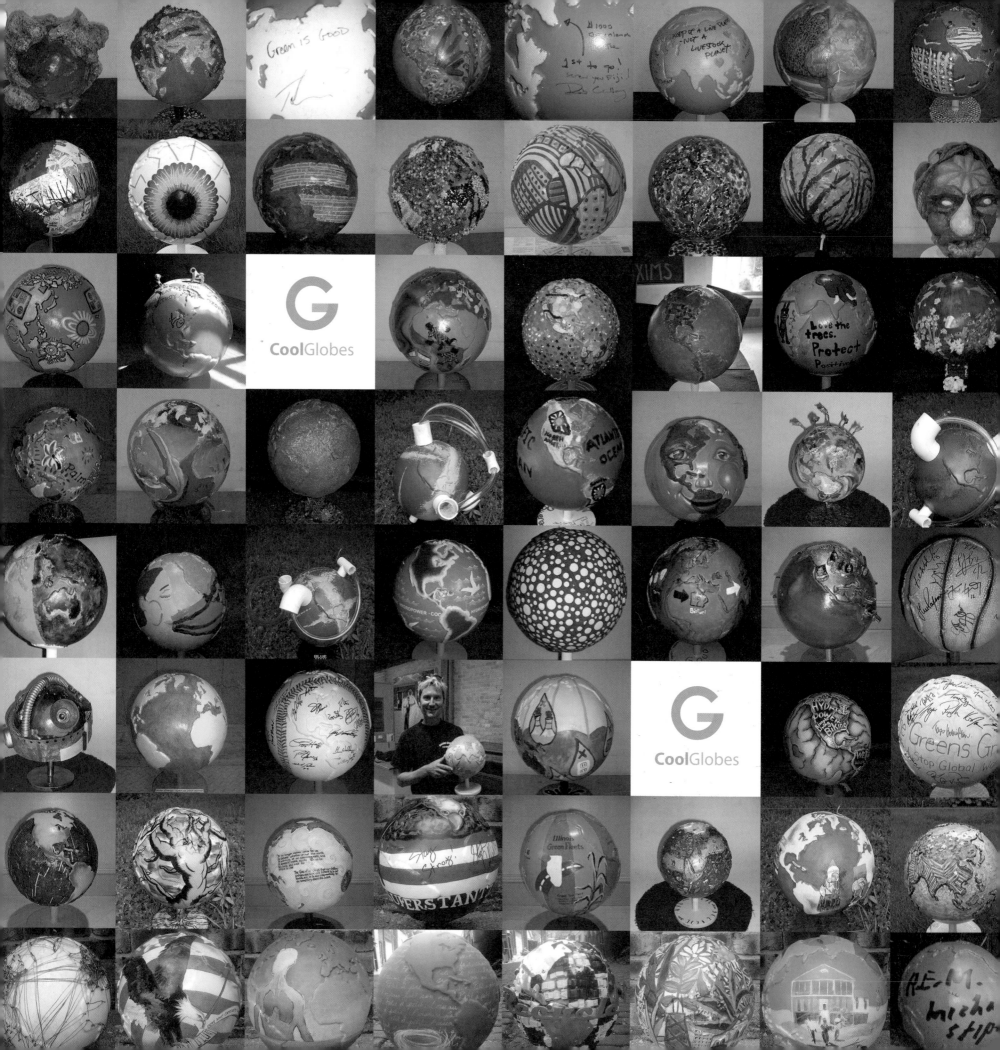